MW00463062

The Street Where the Heart Lies

VOLUME IV IN A NEW

H James H. Heineman New York 1993

The Street Where the Heart Lies

BEMELMANS SERIES

Written and
Illustrated by
Ludwig Bemelmans

ISBN 0-87008-143-8

Printed in the United States of America

First published in this edition
in the United States of America
in 1993

H

James H. Heineman, Inc.,
475 Park Avenue,
New York, NY 10022

This work is within the protectorate of the
Roman D'Amour.

The people here described are neither living nor dead
Nor have they been or are they the bearers of names
used here
Nor tenants in the houses on the street after which
this book is named.

Contents

PART THREE

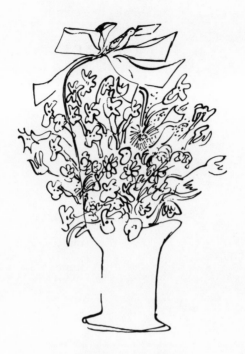

PART ONE

1.

Under the Bridge

"LILY, LILY!" called the old man, the Clochard who was known as King Dagobert. "Look, child, how beautiful!"

From a gift box tied with a silken ribbon, the old man who sat under the bridge took a child's ball, a glowing new, radiant magenta-and-blue-striped ball.

"It's almost too beautiful to play with," said the child.

"It's for your birthday, it's a gift from the Professor." The child held the ball carefully. "Go play with it—it's washable, it's American like the Professor—and you can do with it what you like. Let me see you bounce it."

The child carefully played it against the wall of the bridge. "I will run up and thank him," she said.

"No, no," said King Dagobert, "he doesn't like to be thanked. Just enjoy it."

The old man sat under the bridge on his mattress, next to a decrepit baby carriage. He was a majestic figure with a wiry white beard. He sat leaning against the stone arch, which was tinted a dark burgundy red by the reflection of light. The moisture that rose from the Seine softened all contours and colors. The old man's cloak shone like blue velvet, he wore his hat like a crown.

"Go on now," he said, "good night, little Lily. It's late."

She began bouncing the new ball homeward. She sang out: "Good night, King Dagobert."

She threw her ball against a building that contained the laundry of Madame Bernard and the taxidermist shop of Monsieur Finsterwald, and from there past the window of Madame Carboni, where it always smelled of good cooking. Madame Carboni had a round, shiny, and happy face, a vibrant voice, and next to her always sat her cat Sacha. The cat watched the new ball and put a foot forward, and Madame Carboni, firmly holding him back, said: "What a beautiful new ball. I think I know who gave it to you." Her eyes looked upward to the top of the building whose concierge she was.

The child nodded. "Yes, Monsieur le Professeur gave it to me for my birthday."

Madame Carboni smiled her contentment. As the superintendent of the house she was privileged to look over the mail of her tenants and watch over their comings and goings. She knew what fine mail the Professor had, every day a big batch of it, by air mail from all parts of the world. Even the envelopes that came from Paris were from distinguished addresses, with the postmarks of the most elegant zones of the city, and the packages came from the best shops.

"A gentleman in every sense of the word really, a monsieur always correct," was the way she characterized him. She gave that accolade to few people.

The child bounced the ball on to the Hôtel de France, the ground floor of which was occupied by the commissariat of the police of the district, and then to a house that contained a cabaret called the Relaxez-Vous.

An emaciated bearded musician in sweater and cap, playing on his reedy concertina, sat down on the side of the bridge. He dragged his melancholy Paris air out of the leaky instrument, looking down at the Seine. Some distant explosions sounded like a roll of kettledrums.

The ancient, aching metal mechanism of the clockwork of Notre Dame began its winding and twisting of wires, and the hammer lifted to begin to toll the hour slowly—*bong, bong, bong, bong*. A pause—and then another *bong* to start the count of ten.

Up above, built atop the oldest part of the city, was the Professor's apartment, a modern roost equipped with every comfort and elegance, from whose large windows everything that was beautiful in Paris could be seen, from the gilded figures atop the Cathedral of Notre Dame, to the lighted-up dining room of the Tour d'Argent, over to the tomb of Napoleon, to the Eiffel Tower, to the Champs Elysées, and all the way up to the Sacré Coeur.

Up there, alone, Jeb Clayborn sat at his desk correcting his pupils' papers. He taught at the Lycée Lafayette. He was always cast in seriousness, impatience, and sadness. Walking, talking, even sleeping, he looked disturbed—as many young people do and have always done.

As the bells stopped tolling he got up and walked to the window that looked down on the quay and the Seine. He saw a door open at the cabaret, and from it, as on every evening, came a young woman, pale and very beautiful. She wore an elegant cloak that shone like silver and she had amethysts in her hair. He saw it all clearly, for he was looking at her intently. She stood at the door for a moment and then went back into the cabaret. Now, more lonesome and disturbed than ever, he went back to his work. The musician folded his concertina and left.

From the commissariat came two policemen armed with automatic rifles which they carried on slings and at the ready. At the same time, over the bridge toward them, came the Inspector of the district. And when he met the policemen, the three stopped and saluted each other, and the Inspector looked at his watch.

The policemen stood at attention and said: "All is well."

The Inspector looked pleased. "Nothing to report?"

The older of the two policemen took out his notebook.

"Madame Poupon has sent a color post card from Saint Tropez to her husband. She is still on vacation." The Inspector nodded.

The policeman next pointed up to a large studio window in a very modern apartment with a roof garden and said: "Monsieur Clayborn, the American Professor of literature, stepped into a puddle of water in front of an umbrella shop and when he asked if it had been raining was answered in the affirmative."

"Anything else?"

"Yes, Princess Saroya came from the Cathedral with an escort and they walked around here until their car arrived."

The Inspector asked: "Did you observe anything unusual?"

"No," said the policeman, putting his book away. "They just walked, putting one foot in front of the other."

The Inspector said: "Very good. Continue."

The policemen saluted, turned, and walked back to the commissariat. From under the bridge, the oncoming sound of a motor scooter was heard.

And at that moment, Professor Clayborn appeared at his studio window. He opened the large French windows. He began throwing his possessions out of the studio. First his umbrella, then his statue of Voltaire, and after them his Picasso still life, a vase of flowers, a bowl of fruit, his typewriter and tea service, a reading lamp, an ornamental clock, a traveling bag — and a stack of his pupils' corrected papers which fluttered down like birds.

While this was happening the motor scooter appeared. On it rode the Mother Superior of the Sisters of St. Vincent de Paul. She was a large, kindly woman. Lily ran to her and pointed up to where the Professor was now throwing his cameras and films and books out of the window. Below, the people had assembled, coming from houses and from the cabaret, and the police from the commissariat; Monsieur Finsterwald came from his taxidermist shop, Madame Bernard from her laundry, the Inspector came running over the bridge, and he and the policemen commanded silence.

"Quiet. Calm yourselves. What is going on here?"

The laundress said, wringing her hands: "Poor dear Professor Clay Clay has gone mad."

Lily bounced her ball toward the door where the Professor appeared. He was trying to pull his mattress out of the house. The Professor—gentle, thin, pale—wore an overcoat and sweater and a pair of old gray slacks.

The Inspector of Police said: "You are Professor Clayborn, I believe."

"Yes. Thirty years old, born in New York City, passport No. C042195."

The Inspector, fatherly and with genuine concern, said: "We have all the information, Professor. We know you, but explain to me—"

The Professor held onto his mattress. He said: "I have decided to move under the bridge, to become nobody."

The laundress moaned. "Oh please, stop him! Poor Professor Clay Clay has gone stark mad. Good Lord, there goes my best client. One shirt a day—sometimes two."

The Professor said: "I am sorry, madame, but I have decided—" and he started to drag his mattress toward the bridge.

The laundress held up some linen.

"Professor, not even a sheet—a pillowcase—a towel, a pair of pajamas—a clean shirt for tomorrow?"

The Professor shook his head. "No, thank you, madame. I will sleep on this mattress and cover myself with my coat."

The Mother Superior said: "Let him be."

The little girl had picked up the Professor's umbrella—and the old man, the Clochard known as King Dagobert, was sitting up watching the newcomer arrange his mattress.

The Professor turned to the old man and said: "You permit, monsieur?"

King Dagobert said majestically: "You are welcome."

The Professor turned to the Inspector of Police and asked: "As far as you are concerned, is it permissible for me to take up residence here?"

The Inspector said: "One of the liberties France extends to all is that they may sleep wherever they choose, as long as it doesn't obstruct traffic. You are free to live under any of these bridges."

The little girl placed the umbrella at the head of the Professor's mattress. The Mother Superior said:

"Come, Lily, it is long past your bedtime." She got on her motor scooter and Lily jumped on the small seat in back.

Lily said: "Isn't it wonderful—now King Dagobert is no longer alone—he has a friend."

The people had picked up the various objects: the taxidermist, the typewriter; the laundress, the linen.

The square was empty. The tower of Notre Dame tolled the time. It was the clank clank of heavy metal in wet air and blue night.

"You are not afraid of the dark, I hope?" asked King Dagobert.

"I was once," answered Professor Clayborn. "When I was very little, in America, I woke up alone in bed one night and I was terribly scared. And I got out of bed and ran down the corridor, and there was my nurse's room—she was black—and my father was in bed with her. Since then I have never been afraid of the dark."

2.

Liberty

IN FRONT OF THE STREET LAMP under the bridge, with his head on a box, lay the Clochard, King Dagobert. There was a gust of wind, a burst of rain splashed down. The Professor put up his umbrella.

A policeman stepped under the awning of the taxidermist's shop. Monsieur Finsterwald was working late—his shop was in yellow light. The window glowed like green-silvered glassware, on a bough sat a stuffed weasel. A puma's head looked over one shoulder of the policeman, an owl over his other. The cold rain kept coming down. The policeman shook the rain off his cap.

The taxidermist came out of his shop. He was working on a cat pelt, brushing it in long gentle strokes. He looked haggard and cold—his face was as if made of pale enamel. He turned to the policeman. Pointing at King Dagobert and the Professor, he said: "Look at those fools! There are places for them on nights like this, shelters when it is cold and wet."

The policeman said: "Of course there are, but they don't want to go. They want to be left alone. Good night now, Monsieur Finsterwald, and good rest."

The taxidermist looked down at the Clochard. "I think I would commit suicide if it came to this," he said. "As for you, Professor, I can't understand you at all."

King Dagobert looked up at him with a look of contempt. "Stupid cow," he said, "go away and leave us alone."

The taxidermist said: "Is there anything I can do for you?"

King Dagobert shook himself and motioned him away with his hand. "No thank you," he said. "Go on—go—go home, you will catch the grippe. Eat some warm soup, or better still, drink some hot wine and go to bed." He reached for a bottle and took a deep draft. "You'll catch your death of cold."

"Good night," said the taxidermist as he went into his shop.

The Clochard turned to the Professor.

"You can go up, back into your apartment. Here, take a drink—" He handed him the bottle.

"I feel all aglow and fine," said the Professor. "But I am worried about you. Would you like to go up to my studio? There is some food, and you can warm yourself. I have some dry clothes."

The Clochard said: "You didn't throw everything out?"

"No, I didn't have time. I mean it was sudden, on the spur of the moment."

The Clochard said: "Good. Any wine left up there?"

"Yes," said the Professor, "some good bottles, and brandy, and the icebox is filled with food—sausages, ham, goose liver paste—"

"You have expensive tastes," said the Clochard.

"Do you want me to run up and get you something?" asked the Professor.

"No, no, thank you. I am concerned about you—you are delicate."

"I feel wonderful for the first time in my life—something has happened to me," said Professor Clayborn. "Something really important."

It stopped raining.

The Professor got up. He walked to the embankment and was about to sit down. The Clochard said: "Not on that wet stone—you'll get pneumonia. You always were a sickly child. I remember how they wrapped you up—sweaters, mufflers, and galoshes—"

Clayborn had taken out a cigarette. Now he let the lighter burn on account of his surprise. "But how do you know?" he asked.

"I know your entire family—your father, your uncle John, the old Morgan and his partners, Mr. Chase, your father's lawyer, old Mr. Aubrey Chamber."

Clayborn lit his cigarette. "Who are you?" he asked. He held the lighter close to the Clochard and looked in his face.

The Clochard said: "I was in finance one—in high finance, if you please. Try and remember my voice. Close your eyes and listen to me. I was already old then, and that was some years ago. I was dressed in a resplendent uniform, my chest covered with medals, and your mother spoke to me whenever we met. She had a small dog, and that dog, as most of them do, disliked revolving doors, was afraid of them—and so I always carried him through the door. For people who had large dogs, I un-hooked the door panels and folded them back. We had a great many dog customers. That revolving door, remember it? You helped me push it. Place Vendôme? Does that mean anything? Those memories of early youth usually stick. I had a mustache then—a very well-trimmed mustache and no beard and of course a haircut every Saturday."

Clayborn searched his memory. "A doorman," he said, "and a revolving door—and dear little, long dead Vicky—ah—now I see it clearly. You are Gabriel."

The Clochard said: "I was Gabriel the doorman, at the bank in the Place Vendôme and your family lived across the square at the Ritz."

Clayborn smiled. "You were a very happy man then, as I remember, always smiling, full of jokes—"

"Oh, on the surface I have a sunny nature. But I am like all humans who are not idiots—wretched most of the time. That is, I was. You interrupted a pleasant reverie when you came tonight. I was looking up at the gilded statues of the saints and the angels on the roof of Notre Dame—and thanking them. I had a flash of memory—of my home, of the smells of my wife, the smell of domesticity—that face forever worried, forever pinched, that expression locked in the same grimace of suspi-

13

cion and meanness. I am glad I did it. One cannot always say of the things one does in life, after one has done them, that it was the right thing to do."

Clayborn said: "You have no one—you are all alone?"

"Yes. I did away with her."

"Murder?"

"Oh no, I just left her. Oh how she hated me. That face of resentment that only long years of marriage produces. This loveless creature, who had a half-dozen grimaces for everything in life—one for her pots and pans, another for the ring of the doorbell, for making coffee, for reading the paper, and for me. We had a sweet little girl, that is until she began to talk in that same voice and look at me with that same contempt. And I suppose this condition, as it does in most people's lives, would have continued to be my fate except for what happened.

"It happened like this—like a shot—as if an aggression had been committed. Someone threw a bomb into my life—I didn't have the courage to throw it myself—or to throw myself out of the window like you. I went to jail.

"The jail gate became my door to freedom. It was on account of a beautiful woman," said the Clochard.

"I didn't know one went to jail for that in France—for running away with a woman," said the Professor.

Dagobert said: "One doesn't! I was lucky. It all happened on account of Brigitte Bardot. On account of her I am here today, and a free man."

Clayborn said: "King Dagobert, you are more mysterious than ever."

Dagobert said: "I am a man of a certain age—I am at times a little forgetful. When I worked at the bank, in order not to go home I went to the neighborhood movie house in the street where we lived. I went twice a week. It was there that Miss Bardot appeared in a film called *The Truth*. I paid for my ticket, and always went to the washroom first, and then took my seat. That is when it happened. The young lady who shows people to their seats, and who has a flashlight in her hand, suddenly screamed—because here am I, who has forgotten to do up his trousers, and here are two witnesses who also scream. Somebody blows a whistle, the police come, and I am arrested."

Clayborn asked: "But for what?"

Dagobert said: "Indecent exposure."

Clayborn said: "An accident. And anyway, here in France—"

King Dagobert lifted a finger. "The morality of the bourgeoisie is nowhere higher."

Clayborn asked: "You went to jail?"

"Almost. Ah, the scandal in the street we lived on. The whole neighborhood was inflamed. My wife, pitied, became a martyr.

"Then the police called for me in their infernal way—the wagon stopping in front of the house, two gendarmes leading me to it—and the newspapers carried every word of the story and the trial. It was on radio and television. The whole story and my picture. From that moment on, my wife, my child, were afraid to go out of the house. My picture was next to that of Miss Bardot—in a weekly magazine—Miss Bardot whom I have never met."

"And you lost your position and your pension, poor man, and your family was on the street."

Dagobert sat up. "No no no—on the contrary, miracles happen. The bank is noble, my pension remains. The judge is a most kind and understanding gentleman. He looked across to where my wife was in the courtroom and he must have said to himself: 'That miserable wretch of an ancient doorman! He has served his sentence already—a life sentence! And what comes now will be much harder than jail or the guillotine. I will sentence him to go home.'

"My wife sobbed; her lawyer, over and over again, pointed at her and blubbered: 'Pity! Pity! Behold this poor woman—this poor child!' It was heartbreaking—and I was the villain. The judge however believed me innocent, and said by way of advice: 'Monsieur, go home, buy yourself a television set, put on your pantoufles, and spend your evenings in front of it.'"

"But then how did you get here under the bridge?"

"Because I did not follow the good judge's advice. I walked out of the courtroom—and my wife stood there, with her back toward me, waiting like the police wagon had.

"She had a taxi standing by, the child was glowering, and they were ready to take me home but never to forgive me—to take me into their dreadful custody. And that is when the miracle happened. Somehow I suddenly had the courage to face my enemies. I kissed them both on their cold cheeks and I said:

"'Goodbye, Isabelle, goodbye, Juliette, go back to your respectable neighborhood. Adieu.' I turned my back on them—I waved goodbye.

"I turned the pension over to them and I only wondered at that moment how anyone like me, covered with the medals of two wars, could have been afraid, for a lifetime, of that woman and her daughter."

Clayborn asked: "Had you loved her?"

Dagobert shrugged. "When I was young. When you fall in love with someone, if you love her enough you marry her. I was afraid of lonesomeness—I was like a horse that runs into its stable, even when the stable is on fire. But when I walked away I came to this bridge. I walked over it in the rain."

He stood up—he walked and stretched out his arms.

"I walked and walked over this bridge—back and forth over it. I walked from here to Notre Dame, and then back to the Seine—and suddenly I felt free for the first time in my life. I was without possessions, without care. I also felt richer than all of the people of the international bank of precious metals on the Place Vendôme and their customers for whom I had opened the doors for thirty years."

Clayborn said: "I have often looked down at you from my window up there. I have seen you during the day and night. I have watched you from my studio. Forgive me asking—Lily, Lily, is she your child?"

Dagobert said: "Lily? Oh no, my daughter has been told to forget me. I am sure that the frame in which my picture was in the Rue Tournefort is empty now. No, like the Seine and Notre Dame, and this bridge and all things, that little girl belongs to me. Lily is the child of some people on one of these streets. No one knows who the father is—her mother is working somewhere—and she comes to me—like a bird!"

Clayborn said: "And Miss Bardot, does she give you any more trouble?"

"No," said Dagobert, "I have not been to the movies since. But when I see her face on a poster here and there, I never pass it without giving her my nicest smile, and lifting my hat. People think I'm crazy."

"And how did you get the name—King Dagobert?"

The Clochard pointed to the Relaxez-Vous.

"That one in there discovered who I was. It's on account of him that the whole neighborhood knows, and that I am called King Dagobert. In the beginning it was rather awkward. For a while children ran after me and cried, 'Dagobert — Dagobert — here comes King Dagobert.' Then they got tired of it."

"What does it mean?" asked the Professor.

"There once was a king by that name in France. His clothes were always in disorder, and he never buttoned his trousers. There is a song about it."

3.

Perfect Service

THE BELLS OF NOTRE DAME struck eleven.

"I dream of restaurants sometimes," said the King. "That is perhaps the only thing I miss in my former life—the neighborhood bistro—a place called Chez Armand, very unpretentious, and nothing to brag about by way of kitchen. But it was a refuge for me then, chiefly because there was nobody there who made me suffer. Friends were around me, and the specialty of the house was the gigot aux flageolets; the Algerian red wine was served in cloudy glasses, but I found some peace there. Anyway

I got away from the family—from my wife's casseroles and the eternal stale smell of domesticity."

The Professor said: "With me restaurants had the opposite effect. I suffered in them—especially in those of the first grand de luxe category."

"I passed the Restaurant Lucas Dubuffet today," said King Dagobert. "I inhale the perfume of that kitchen with much pleasure. It's clean—one can look inside—they keep a good table."

"That was my father's favorite eating place," said the Professor. "He had a very small list of restaurants—Maxim's, le Grand Vefour, a few more three-star places. That's all he ever went to, and he liked Lucas Dubuffet most of all."

"I don't blame him, I could be tempted to go there myself."

"We always went there the first night for dinner whenever my father came to Paris, and also the last night when he left.

"Meals with the family were always a disaster. Toward the end of my father's life they became terrifying, silent sessions. Nobody spoke, for every word somehow provoked my father to outbursts.

"In ordering meals, as in everything else in his life, he decided on what was to be eaten. He had a curious way of ordering, that is he consulted no one's wishes. He avoided looking at anyone and especially at me. Occasionally he shot a glance at the men taking the order, which was always the same group—the proprietor, the headwaiter, and the wine waiter.

"Mostly he ordered the meal past the right side of my face and the wines—because the sommelier usually stood in back of my chair—to the left side of me. I did my best to avoid looking at my father. We were both experts at ignoring each

20

other. I looked at the glasses, the flowers, the silverware, at my mother.

"I also avoided looking at Mr. Chamber, his friend, his steady companion, the one person toward whom my father leaned and with whom he had long whispered conversations.

"Mr. Chamber was a florid man. I had seen him once in his bathing suit in Deauville. He had an immense chest and under it curious girl-like legs. Dressed he was the perfect image of an American executive. You could have put his face on a fifty-dollar savings certificate. Everything connected with my father had a feeling of money about it — except me. Mr. Chamber was a silent, strong man, who had at one time in his youth swum around Manhattan and still believed in long walks, deep breathing, and noncompetitive sports. He led the clean life up to five o'clock, when, under the great pressure of his tremendous corporate responsibilities, he started to drink heavily. They both drank well and ate everything the doctor had told them was bad for them. They had contempt for all and everything — labor unions, doctors, the French, me, my mother, the President of the United States, the fact that people could vote, the fact that women had the vote. As for women, there had never been the slightest scandal or even the faintest breath of it, as far as both my father and C. Aubrey Chamber were concerned. That may also have been out of contempt for women. They were both married to gentle, kind, and beautiful women, whom they took for granted and treated with a peculiar form of tolerance, a vicious, icy, mostly polite brutality. Every word was loaded with some sort of reproach, insult, or superiority and indifference. It had become chronic, it had always been so ever since I remember having learned to understand speech.

"About the only time I saw them smile together was when some stock they did not own suddenly went down.

"My poor mother suffered in silence. She sat there among the snobbish patronage, attended by the old headwaiters, captains, and waiters, all of whom seemed to have a peculiar loathing for their clientele.

"My father was one of the best customers. He said the food was superb, and also the service. I suppose it was.

"The last night we were there was a special occasion. My father asked the proprietor and chef to order the dinner — he wanted something unusual, a bon voyage dinner on the occasion of his departure for America. I can tell you exactly what we had. It started with everything by way of hors d'oeuvres; then came caviar with blinis, after that a tray of assorted oysters, turtle soup, trout cooked in champagne, followed by capon; then sorbet of wild strawberries; then woodcock, asparagus, and after that goose liver with truffles, soufflé, ice cream, cookies, and fruit."

"They left out the cheese," said the Clochard.

"No, no, I forgot the cheese. That is they came with a wagon with cheeses, a hundred varieties of the best in France, and you could have some if you wanted to, but nobody wanted any. All of the food was eaten in total silence among a décor of flowers and a view of the thick necks of people at other tables which I saw in the tilted mirror overhead.

"Most of the women wore limp hats and dressed in a very special kind of expensive squalor. The men were all heavy, designed for the oversize chairs and banquettes of the room, and all had their special places reserved and always ate at the same tables. In that mirror I could also see the buffet with pyramids of food, the crystal chandeliers, and the obese, unpleasant servitors with bulging eyes, continuously shuffling back and forth and back and forth. I could watch the entry of the arthritic clientele with their grunts and groans, the wine buckets being carried past the obscene faces of most of the men and women who were busily talking about the others in the room . . . the jewels, the hairdos. I also saw the lovely things in this room—the maroon-colored interior edged with gold, the cut-glass partitions to protect the clientele from drafts, the brass fixtures, and the ceiling which looked like old ivory.

"All of it was bright, immaculately dusted and polished, the nearby objects very clearly visible, those in the distance as in a painting. The women were very much like one sees in Renoir or Degas paintings, only doubly lovely. But no matter how much I wanted to turn around, to look at them directly, to gaze at this or that beautiful face, I could merely watch in the mirror, and even then not openly but only by sweeping casual glances. Here and there I saw a man of a certain age seated with a gem-laden woman of great allure, and the woman would flash an occasional inquiry to me by way of a look, via the mirror. But I am very uncommunicative and not cut out for romance, and I always had to look away. I could not stand the direct saber thrust of love, much as I desired it. I was—I am—an idiot in these matters, afraid to take a step. My hands get moist like a schoolboy's. I worship from afar.

"I sat silent through the whole meal at our table. We were like the French families with their still, straightsitting, serious children who do not even swing their legs, but sit through these endless meals, and eventually sit on the other side of these same tables with their own children. This restaurant had a tradition.

Into the grillwork on the windows the figures 1845 were worked. That is the year it was established.

"Among the details I observed was the serving of wine. The sommelier poured a little of the wine into my father's glass, and then held his bottle with an 'I dare you to complain' look. He had eyes like plover's eggs, which lay in a cinnamon-colored sacking of flesh, and his nose was blue-veined from self-sacrifice in wine tasting. My father was a match for him, however. His arrogance was perfected to the smallest detail. He kept the wine waiter hanging. He tasted the wine slowly, and then, putting the glass back on the table, gave no sign of pleasure, recognition, or appreciation, not even a nod of thanks or grunt of assent for its submission to his judgment. The fact that he did not send it back was enough, though, and the sommelier then poured it into the glasses of the people at the table—into Baccarat glasses so fine that when you squeezed them the round bottom became slightly oval.

"A trio played a carefully selected instrumental accompaniment to all this. The chef came to the table. Mr. Chamber nodded and thanked him.

"The cloud of blue smoke overhead, the overheated room, the smell of food—it was enough to make one sick. And still my father sat there, and stared ahead of him, and next to him sat C. Aubrey Chamber, and he also stared. One of my brothers, the middle one of the three who had made good, sat next to me. My mother's unhappy eyes wandered about the scene as mine did. Occasionally people came in, occasionally people paid and went out. The musicians went out for a rest and came back, and the leader of the orchestra stood at our table and began to play for us. My mother smiled pleasantly at him. My father stared.

Mr. Chamber handed some money to the fiddler so my father would not be disturbed. The musician bowed and left. The room began to get cool. The service here was really excellent, for although excepting for a few others we were the only party left, the waiters made no motion of clearing off the buffet, or closing up. They stood patiently here and there with arms folded, staring into space.

"The wine waiter never went through the wine-tasting ritual with champagne. It was taken for granted that champagne, like Coca-Cola, was even in quality from bottle to bottle. The waiter merely served as many bottles as he felt were needed. He twisted another cork silently out of a bottle. In one of her few gestures of revolt, my mother always turned the wine glasses at her place upside down at the very beginning of the meal, and only left the water glass standing. The music kept playing. The headwaiter came several times and asked if everything was all right, and then backed away.

"We were still waiting when my father moved a little—he made a sound—it was like a sigh. The other guests all had gone by now. We were the last ones left. My mother sat still as always. I looked at my father—his color had changed. I got up, I told my brother to take Mother to the hotel and send the car back for Father. I walked out toward the door. I told the proprietor of the restaurant to call a doctor. I went back. Mr. Chamber sat still next to my father. We waited—my father sometimes fell asleep at the table, as did Mr. Chamber, and they could sit forever. The doctor came and touched my father. He sat down comfortably on the deep upholstery of that restaurant. He took hold of him by both his massive shoulders. My father's head tilted forward a little. He was dead.

"Mr. Chamber was asleep. I don't know whether this happened regularly in this restaurant, but I must say that the service was perfect to the end. Two men came, and taking hold of my father, one on the left and one on the right, sort of walked him out. I felt guilty about being without emotion. A melancholy wave rushed over me.

"I felt a sorrow for all the uselessness of this life, a compassion for all, even the greedy, discontented servitors.

"The proprietor stood in his usual posture and place near the door, with the 'bon soir, monsieur-dames' and the 'merci' expression on his face; his slightly tilted face bore the usual complications of farewell, goodbye, and au revoir, and was suited perfectly to the grave adieu. So were the faces of all his maîtres d'hôtel, captains, and waiters, who had no need to change any of their miserable expressions which were in perfect accord with the end, with the departure of the esteemed client.

"It was a play without beginning or end, of figures moving to and fro. It was not without humor. When the crocque-morts had come into the room with their black gloves they were for a moment undecided whom to pick up—whether it was C. Aubrey Chamber or my father—for the other looked as dead and gone as did my father. He was drunk and staring. The maître d'hôtel pointed out the one to be removed.

"The limousine had come back and now it stood below and the two men took him down, as if he were a little under the weather. The cloakroom girl, whose name was Mireille, brought his coat and his American businessman's hat, and put them into the car. It went off. I went upstairs. Two captains helped Mr. Chamber down the stairs. It was so perfectly done that the doorman was confused and said to me as we loaded Mr. Chamber into a taxi:

"'I trust there's nothing wrong with Monsieur Chamber.'

"I said, 'No, no, don't worry, he's all right.'

"Well, my father's battle was over. I went up to tell the headwaiter to add the tips to the bill and send it to the hotel.

"My father had always threatened to cut me out of his will. The will was opened by Mr. Chamber the next day, and either my father had not gotten around to it, or else he hadn't meant to—at any rate, I suddenly had more money than I ever expected to have. We went back to New York for the funeral. My mother died soon after."

"And Mr. C. Aubrey Chamber?"

"Oh, he is still sitting and staring at the same restaurant interiors. One doesn't know if he is alive or dead. At his side is his ever-patient and beautiful dear wife—patiently waiting."

"For him to die?"

"No. Strangely enough she loves him.

"One more thing I must tell you about the perfect service at the Restaurant Lucas Dubuffet. Only after I had signed the bill and said good night to the proprietor and all the maîtres d'hôtel and waiters, only after that was the signal given to clear off and they all went into action to cart off the buffet, remove the linen, put the chairs on the tables, and start turning out the lights."

"What was that menu again? Please tell me once more," asked King Dagobert.

"Oh, the bon voyage menu. I know it by heart and will never forget it.

"First: Hors d'oeuvres.

"Then: Caviar de sterlet with blinis.

"After: Assorted oysters served like a wedding cake in a large batch on ice. You chose what you wanted: Les fines claires, those that are boat-shaped, and which I prefer, then those that are flat with a slightly metallic taste, then the Belons, and those from England. My father would eat a dozen of these at least.

"Then: Clear turtle soup.

"Then: Trout cooked in champagne.

"Followed by the specialty of the house: capon cooked à la demi-deuil—in half mourning—an effect produced by slipping thin slices of truffles between the skin and the flesh and this further enhanced by a sauce flavored with morilles. Very good that, I must say. With that a purée of mushrooms.

"By way of a break there was served a corbet of wild strawberries au Grand Marnier and then we started eating seriously again.

"Flaming woodcock, with its long beak and the skull with its hollow eyes left on, as well as its gray bird legs, and this accompanied by Egyptian quails, little sparrowlike creatures.

"With this les asperges de France served lukewarm with vinaigrette.

"The médaillons of goose liver with truffles.

"A pause and a change of table linen. They rolled a new tablecloth across, transferring personal belongings, candlesticks, centerpiece, et cetera, the way they make beds in a hospital where they roll the patient from one side to the other. New glasses, new napery, new silverware. Now the third act of the art of eating at table began.

"The soufflé de Grenade à l'Orientale.

"Biscuit glacé aux violettes.

"The tray of petits fours.

"The basket of fruit: nectarines, raisins, hothouse grapes, hothouse peaches, cherries, apricots.

"The tray with liqueurs.

"The fingerbowls.

"The cigars.

"The matches—special kitchen matches."

"You have made me hungry, and again, you have forgotten the cheeses," said the Clochard, who had been pensively picking his teeth while listening. He groaned and getting up reached from the edge of his mattress into the baby carriage for the bottle of cheap wine and the crust of bread.

"I have nothing against cheese," said the Professor. "I still have some fine Brie up there, I haven't thrown everything out. I'll hop upstairs. In the icebox there are all kinds of food left, and some wine, and that Brie—"

"Don't bother," said the King. "With an empty stomach one has incredible imagination. I am just starting with that menu all over—we are at the flaming woodcock—" He sniffed pleasantly with closed eyes and held the bottle under his nose.

"Well, a flaming woodcock, I am sorry, I could not supply for you this instant."

"Therefore consider the advantage of the imagination," said the King, blinking and wiping his lips with the back of his hand.

4.

Sleepless Night

THE BELLS OF NOTRE DAME struck twelve. The door of the cabaret opened and from it came a luminous creature in a long, trailing ermine cloak, a diamond coronet, and bird of paradise feathers in her hair. She came forward in elegant rhythm—as the young, when playful, free, and unobserved, walk in extravagant harmony of limbs, face, and motion. She had clusters of jewels sparkling at her throat and wrists and at the tips of her small, golden slippers. She came down toward the embankment and sat down near the mattress on which the Professor lay. She leaned against the lamppost. The Professor sat up. She glittered like the evening star. The Professor turned and crept forward. She took a cigarette out of a pack, inclined herself toward him, and asked:

"Light?"

He reached into his pocket and brought forth a golden, expensive lighter. A flame shot out.

"This hardly goes with my present mode of living," he said. "It's yours."

She shielded the flame with her hands and said:

"Burn my skin if you will. I don't mind. But be careful of my furs. If you burn a hole in them, my husband will be furious. I would never hear the end of it. Can't you sleep?"

The Professor said: "I was almost asleep when you came. I thought I was having a beautiful dream, and I must tell you, awake or dreaming, that this is the most wonderful and exciting moment in my life. Do you live here, madame?"

She said: "Yes, I live right there, where the music comes from. I get up when you go to bed. I live at night, mostly."

"I lived during the day in that house. I am Professor Clayborn, that is, I was until a while ago. Now I am nobody, an indigent. I have changed my life."

She said: "It takes courage. It's like dying and being born again."

The Professor said: "It seems like that, wonderfully so."

"What made you do it?"

"I couldn't stand myself any more."

"For any particular reason?"

The Professor said: "Well, they all seemed very important

31

and good reasons until now. Now that I have freed myself of my former existence they don't seem so terribly important any more. My former self is what I was discontented with."

She said: "I too felt that way. I always wanted to move, to see the world, and we traveled, Monsieur Corti—that is my husband—and I. And now I don't want to travel any more. I want to stay. I am an artiste. We traveled to London, to Monte Carlo, to Vienna, as far as Istanbul and Madrid, but I like Paris best. Monsieur Corti says that anyone who leaves the sight of the Place de la Concorde or Notre Dame is a fool. 'What's the use of traveling when you are already there,' he says. He says clever things like one reads in books."

The Professor said: "He's right, and very intelligent, your husband."

"He is, and a great man, and very elegant, and handsome—and insanely jealous. He hardly ever lets me out of his sight. He watches over me constantly. I am never alone, even when I get a massage. He has engaged a masseur because he is very proud of my figure. He sits there, my husband, while I have this massage and he watches, and he knows exactly what is a massage and what is not, and when that masseur gets a little affectionate with his hands, then he is there, and he shows his teeth like a watchdog."

The Professor said: "I can't blame him."

She smiled. Her jewelry shone: rubies, emeralds, diamonds in her hair, on her wrists, at her throat. The Professor gazed at her in wonderment.

"I warn you," she said, laughing, "he is ready to die for me."

King Dagobert, who had been sitting quietly like an icon in his niche, came forward and handed a small package to Gala.

"Thank you, good King Dagobert," she said, and opened it, and bit into the sandwich.

"This is my lifesaver," she said.

"He starves the poor little creature to death, to keep her beautiful," said the old man as he handed her the bottle.

She lifted it and drank, and the King moved back in the shadows.

She inhaled deeply and said: "This is one of my rare moments off. My husband doesn't mind me seeing King Dagobert. I come down here between shows. Now we are rehearsing a new show. Wish me luck."

"All the luck there is," said the Professor.

"So far all goes well. Monsieur Corti has big plans. He is very artistic, always dreaming up new scenes, new tableaux. Art means even more than I do to him."

The Professor said: "Your husband seems very romantic."

Gala said: "Yes, he is a great man."

The Professor said: "I hope to have the honor of meeting him some time."

She said: "He discovered me. I had no talent, he told me I didn't, and I believed him. But talent can be beaten into one, like into dogs you see on the stage. He said I had a marvelous bone construction—he loves phrases like that—and of course he could see the bones when he found me. I was fourteen then. He taught me acrobatic dancing and acting, and ballroom dancing, and then stripping—which is a great art, Professor, let no one tell you different—and one thing Miomo Corti knows is how to take clothes off women, and how to teach them to take them off themselves. He was at one time the greatest impresario of the world. He controlled all the Alhambras and Moulin

Rouges and Palace Theaters. Then he lost it all and his debts were so great he had to keep moving. That's when he met me and that's when I saw the world, on one-night stands. And when I was taught—fast—I danced. I starved, I was locked up and slapped around until my head whirled. He was a perfectionist, and he was jealous. I couldn't look at another man, I was not allowed to go to the cinema alone. At the hairdresser he sat under the next drier reading. But he got me jobs, one after the other and better and better. Then he married me and he never let me forget that either. I wasn't to look at anyone else, I was helpless, and still I was a woman, and young. There was a time when I started to hate him and all men, but slowly I changed. Now I don't hate him any more.

"In those four minutes that I stand nude before the audience—that is my moment. I know I am more beautiful than all the others. And when I do the act that he taught me so well, when I drop all, I watch their faces, their eyes and open mouths. When I see the men, their faces more naked than my body, and the women they have with them, envious and their eyes filled with cold hatred, that is when I have my exaltation. Do you understand that?"

The Professor said: "Frankly no, I have never seen such a performance. Have you ever tried to get away from him?"

"I tried once. He threatened to kill himself, and he almost did. I came back at the last moment. So—that is the story of my life. I, too, wanted to change it, but then I didn't any more."

The Professor asked: "Is there anything you want terribly badly?"

Gala said: "Yes, to install a bath. That is the only thing I miss. This old house in which we live has one toilet for forty people."

The Professor looked up at his apartment. "Any time that you want," he said, "you can take a bath up in my apartment."

"Oh, Miomo would be furious."

"What do you do now?"

"The kind Mother Superior allows me to bathe in the convent."

She got up. She stood under the street lamp, radiant and luxurious as a young queen. She said:

"I'd better get back, or else there will be a crisis when Miomo gets back and finds me with you."

"You are lovely," stammered the Professor. "Magnificence itself."

She laughed. "It's an illusion. It comes all out of thrift shops, and it's all secondhand or stolen. My fur coats are all false, other animals than they pretend to be: muskrats, goats, and rabbits. I always have my nostrils filled with fur hairs. And the jewelry is glitter, cheap stuff you hang on a Christmas tree. You know, I don't have a thing to wear. I have to wait until it's night to go out, and then I can't take anything off, for look—"

She opened her cloak and she was naked under it.

"I have nothing under the skin of these animals except this G string—that's another specialty of Miomo Corti. He has a friend, Monsieur Finsterwald the taxidermist there, who stuffs dogs and also prepares cat skins for rheumatic people. And when he finds a fur—a marmalade cat, or a golden tabby—then he cuts that up and I wear that as a G string in the act, and that's really the only clothes that I can say he buys me. I attach it to my skin with the stuff men use to keep their toupees on. Oh, he thinks of everything, my husband. How to pose a girl to excite the audience—how to warm up a French crowd at fifty new

francs admission. That takes doing. He knows his business."
She twisted her body and did a few elegant poses, and she
slipped on the stone.

The Professor, who was in a state of adoration, tried to catch
her—he enfolded her knees—and they both fell and rolled
down the incline.
She said:

"Pardon me."
He asked:

"Are you hurt?"
She said:

"No."
He said:

"Sorry."
She said:

"It was an accident."
He said:

"Of course, for I would never have had the courage to
embrace you in a thousand years."

She kissed him.

"How touching," said a voice from above.

A debonair figure, leaning on his cane, stood there smiling.

"My husband, Miomo Corti," said Gala.

5.

The Rehearsal

As with most Parisian theaters and places of entertainment, the Relaxez-Vous was a firetrap crammed with uncomfortable chairs and small tables. It was Miomo Corti's conviction that the spectators were most receptive and content when they sat on top of one another with barely enough elbow room to applaud. Fresh air cut into the mood of a show. There was no proper heating in the low-ceilinged room, except that which came from the bodies of the performers and the audience, and when the crowds came it would turn into a humid hothouse and become cozy. Up to then it was cold.

Now it was icy cold. Madame Michel, whose face in the light of day was like a Kokoschka portrait, painted in smeary theatrical make-up and with hair the color of sulfur and copper, was working in a sweater and corduroy slacks, the ends of which were stuffed into lamb's-wool-lined boots. She was on the small stage hammering planks in place and moving properties.

Madame Michel, a small intense person, was a pillar of integrity. She had a direct approach to life and able, strong hands. She had a heavy hammer and nails that could penetrate masonry, bricks, or stone. The old building was solidly put together and it took hard blows to put the spikes in place. Madame Michel hammered and then hooked onto the wall an immense imitation Greuze nude in a heavy frame, and the stuffed head of a moose. The painting was from the police, who stored fake works of art in a warehouse and once a year auctioned them off. The moose was on loan from the taxidermist Finsterwald.

Also hanging from the ceiling and the walls were halberds, ancient tubas, a kettledrum, helmets of various regiments, and the skin of a zebra. This versatile collection of objects, which had nothing to do with one another or with what was happening on the stage, had, according to Miomo Corti, the effect of making the audience feel immediately at home and absorbing their attention during pauses, "giving them something to look at."

During the day Madame Michel was busy every minute from early morning on. She carried out cases of empty bottles, garbage pails, swept the sidewalk, scrubbed the floor. She was wardrobe woman, scenery painter and stagehand, an excellent cook and seamstress. At night when the show started, she performed a miracle by turning herself into an artiste.

In grandiose follies of velvet and silk, in feather boas, in net stockings and high-button shoes, padded all over and in towering coiffures and long gloves, she performed as Yvette Guilbert, a living Toulouse-Lautrec portrait of the famous music hall singer. She pranced out and confronted her audience with joyous insolence. If they were naked of face and self-protective and silent in the presence of the nude Gala, they relaxed at the entry of Madame Michel. The snobs smiled, the superior became simple, the aristocrats became common, all dropped their reserve. She had them in her hand as long as she wanted them. At the end of her songs there was always roaring applause for more. She was of the good old golden days. Oh Paris, oh beauty, oh kisses, perfume and flowers — and when it finally came to an end the audience reached for her like children begging for another good night kiss from Mommy before it was over, and the world sank back into darkness. She was a drug against loneliness, she pushed away melancholy sadness. And as was the beauty of Gala, so was the art of Madame Michel a defense against the constant fear of death that is in all humans.

After she had moved the piano and nailed down the planks, Madame Michel covered the stage with a ground cloth, adjusted various spotlights, and arranged a comfortable chair on a platform on the right, a place designated as the royal box on which people of special prominence would be seated.

Miomo Corti came down the circular stairs majestically. He had a face on which he wore several masklike expressions; it seemed distinguished, for the first few moments, when one came upon it. The skin was dark brown with flashes of blue, the eyes deep set and of awesome directness, especially when he was in pursuit of an object. When he relaxed, when he got tired, the register of failure lay on his face. He was in pursuit now, twisting the handle of his stick. Then he tapped with it and impatiently called for Gala. She came running—and the orchestra of the Relaxez-Vous, which consisted of a turntable and four blaring loud-speakers, went into action and the rehearsal began. It lasted for hours. Gala had to go through the routines over and over. Corti demanded perfection.

The process of Gala denuding on stage was a ritual, a traditional ceremonial to Corti which he took as seriously as the Academician took the Encyclopaedia and the Institut de France, the patriot his flag or the "Marseillaise."

He worked with Gala's pelvis and firm round bosoms as did other Frenchmen with their materials—as charcutiers, displaying delicious cuts of meat on marble slabs—as pâtissiers, squeezing icing on cakes—as painters or dressmakers—with the passionate zeal that makes people say of the French that they are different from all other races in the world. He got the most out of the ultimate possible, and every time.

He composed erotic ballets and until the sublime creature—the object of his artistry—twisted, moved, did every gesture precisely right, it was done over and over again and again. The process was cruel. It had started on that day at noon, which was early morning for Corti; there had been four hours of rehearsal now. Gala was hungry but there was no letup. Miomo Corti tapped his stick to give the signal for the next act, to the music of Chopin and the words of Baudelaire, which he recited. She would do a scene called "Le Mort Joyeux."

He put the record on the player and started to recite, and Gala came from the wings. Madame Michel said:

"That poor girl can't work on air. Give her something to eat. Let me cook a plate of soup or something. Just one little thin chop," she pleaded. "Look at her—this child is like a half-starved kitten; she has to get some food into her."

"You have a lot to attend to," said the impresario. He paced up and down.

"I love to attend to the kitchen," said Madame Michel and went to the small oven.

Miomo Corti wore a black turtle-neck sweater and he conducted like von Karajan, with modeling, precise gestures, intense and merciless, until he got what he wanted. The body of Gala was his instrument, his orchestra.

"Don't make the mistake," he said in his nasal, lecturing tone, "that this is amusement. I have told you a thousand times, and must repeat it again, that it is dead serious. Just look at the faces of the spectators when you perform at a sacred rite. If this is destroyed, then we fail miserably."

Madame Michel was cooking and Gala listened to the sizzling of the chop. She liked meat, when she got any, medium rare. Madame Michel took some mashed potatoes, which were strictly forbidden, and smeared them flat on the plate so that Corti would not notice them. Then she placed the chop on top of this paste and, with a look of gratitude, Gala wolfed it down.

Miomo Corti gave her no peace. "You come on stage to my words, listen—" He tapped the rhythm. "You come on as an old woman, covered with moldy material—listen to me, stop eating:

Dans une terre grasse et pleine d'escargots
Je veux creuser moi même une fosse profonde.

"Now you begin to défeuiller—the leaves fall off you. You must feel the escargots, the smeary, slimy escargots."

"Ah, des escargots," said Madame Michel. "Who wants escargots?"

"Quiet," snapped Miomo Corti. "I am not talking about food, I am talking of the escargots of Baudelaire." Madame Michel excused herself.

"Let's get on with it. Have you finished? Take your place. Remember you are dead in a graveyard. Oh oh oh, don't swallow, don't burp. Now—music—and listen—" His voice was hollow, haunting, a crepuscular recitative.

"Dans une terre grasse et pleine d'escargots . . . Gala, this is the first time you have come on stage with Einfühlung, with feeling for the role." Gala stood barefoot and in the mantle of moldlike material to which a few gilded autumn leaves had been attached. She wore pale make-up.

It was now almost four-thirty, and time to prepare the coffee for the entire Commissariat de Police—a public relations effort of Miomo Corti to keep the neighboring officials on good terms with the Relaxez-Vous.

Madame Michel watched the coffee machine. Then she got a mop and said, "Excuse me, please," and moved a screen in the rear of the establishment. She opened the door to the lavatory and turned on the gaslight. It was primitive but very clean, of tile—a place to the left for men, another to the right for the ladies—with a mirror and a small table with a sign on it that said "Merci" for any tips left there by visitors.

Miomo Corti tapped his stick with impatience, Gala got into position, once more the turntable music started. Corti began to recite the poem, and he went on to the second time where Gala dropped the mantle and revealed herself as the young and joyous dead maiden.

The street door opened and a dog came in — not walking on the floor but at the height of a man's waist, as if floating, a little white-and-black dog, a fox terrier, shaking and swaying. He stood on a small board and as he approached one could see that his feet had been nailed to the board.

"Bon soir, bon soir," said the taxidermist, Monsieur Finsterwald, looking smaller than usual in spite of the shawls and sweaters he was wearing.

At the sight of the dog, whose lifelike appearance baffled even Miomo Corti, Gala broke out in tears and sobbing. She cried:

"Ton-Ton — !"

Madame Michel came running from the washroom. Gala kissed the small dog and petted him.

"It's for you," Monsieur Finsterwald said to Gala. He also handed her his handkerchief to dry her tears.

"Oh dear Lord," said Gala. "Look at him, Miomo, just as he was in life."

"Yes, remarkable," said Miomo Corti impatiently. The record was stopped and Monsieur Corti fixed the taxidermist with a cold stare. "We are rehearsing," he said. "I expect someone important any minute now." Gala held onto her little stuffed dog. The taxidermist handed a pack of photographs to Gala and said:

"I did not need any of these. I remembered him so well; he

visited me in my shop almost daily." Corti took Ton-Ton from Gala and placed him on the bar.

"A masterpiece of taxidermy," said Miomo Corti with finality.

"Yes, look at his eyes," said the taxidermist. "It took me a month to find the right shade—one was green, the other brown. And the expression around the mouth—you remember how Ton-Ton always smiled?"

"Exactly the way he did in life."

"Thank you, thank you, Monsieur Finsterwald, and adieu." Gala broke out anew in tears.

Madame Michel said: "May I offer you something, Monsieur Finsterwald? A cup of coffee?" She looked at the clock. "In a little while it will be coffee time. We have made an arrangement with the Commissariat de Police next door, and at five they come and get twelve mugs of coffee. I always start the machine at a quarter to five and I'll make a little more, an extra cup."

"Madame Michel," said Miomo Corti sharply, "we have but twelve mugs. I am trying to rehearse, I expect Signor Vivanti. Please don't drive me crazy." Monsieur Corti had taken the taxidermist by the arm and was steering him toward the door. "I will have a ticket for you, for the opening of the new show, Monsieur Finsterwald, but just now everything is upset and going wrong. Excuse me, please."

"Yes," said Madame Michel to Finsterwald, who looked at Gala assuming her starting pose again. "You must forgive us, everything is upside down today. I am sorry. And the police, they are difficult, they want it fresh and hot and exactly on time. It is always a tricky business to do favors for the police."

Miomo Corti started the music again. Gala came forward as Corti recited.

To gain an extra moment's beholding of her beauty, the taxidermist remained with his hand on the doorknob.

"Yes, the police. Poor fellows, they need sympathy and something hot, especially at a time like this when the weather is going crazy, as is the whole world, and policemen are being shot at like pigeons by terrorists."

"Will you please leave!" screamed Miomo Corti. The taxidermist went.

"A true artist," said Madame Michel, "to bring dear little Ton-Ton back to life."

Upon these words, Gala broke out in tears anew.

Miomo Corti hit the table in front of him with his stick and cursed, and said to Madame Michel:

"Shut your trap, old canaille, and get on with your work. Oh God, what a day!"

Madame Michel placed each of the twelve coffee mugs on the ugly messhall tray with a bang, and into each she threw a spoon, and snapped her eyes at Corti.

The impresario insisted on absolute silence during his séances, and especially during rehearsals of such somber works as "Le Mort Joyeux." He waited for it now. And slowly he got it.

Rolls-Royces are silent too, excepting for their electric clocks, and one of them was ticking outside the door of the Relaxez-Vous.

"It's him," said Madame Michel. "He is here."

She had seen the big car arrive.

6.

Save Himself Who Can

FROM THE ROLLS-ROYCE stepped Vittorio Vivanti, the little giant, the human volcano, a Milanese millionaire, without a neck, and the head of a tadpole, a sensuous mouth running from ear to ear, a well-nourished man, his storm-tossed face scarred by lifelong battle. He was a bulging compact man, his eyes bulging from their sockets, his hands on short arms bulging from his jacket, his short legs carrying him forward on small feet in thin Italian shoes. He ran rather than walked, and ran as if he feared to fall with the weight of his upper structure. He embraced his old friend while looking about at the curious place, taking measure of the house, the neighborhood, the people, and then he stumbled inside in haste. He almost ran head-on into the moose; he was baffled by the decor.

"How many can you seat here?" he asked.

"Two hundred comfortably," said Miomo Corti. He was led to the reserved table in the front row. Madame Michel brought a bucket with champagne and twisted the cork out of it expertly. Miomo Corti poured two glasses; they touched them and Signor Vivanti toasted his host and wished him good fortune. Corti answered him in Italian. He was in his element, he knew his business. Miomo Corti tapped his cane for absolute silence. Madame Michel attended to the turntable. Corti said:

"Let's try 'Les Plaisirs Clandestins.'" The loud-speakers scratched and then the Chopin melody began for the hundredth turning that day, and Corti closed his eyes and started to recite another of his creations:

> Fermes, en un soir
> d'automne
> Je respire l'odeur de
> ton sein chaleureux—

Gala, now in a diaphanous costume, had come on scene. The projectors were on her. Signor Vivanti leaned forward and his face took on the look of pain and longing which women of great beauty produce.

This one especially inflicted the most severe pain and longing. He stood on the trembling soil of passion. He was attacked, shot, captured. As her garments loosened, his eyes almost bulged out of his head, his pulse raced, a kind of percussion started in his skull. He had high blood pressure and he had to be careful. He leaned back. During a calm passage, a glissando to muted violins, as the last of her covering slid to the ground, floating down as a guirlande of golden autumn leaves—an explosion took place outside.

Madame Michel was back in the washroom. She had just wiped clean the saucer that stood in front of the sign on which was lettered "Merci" when she heard more shots and the Relaxez-Vous was shaken by a bomb which detonated close by. In a swirl of rain, two Arab terrorists came flying into the room, both armed with revolvers and burp guns, and looking desperately for a place to hide.

Wild eyed, and pursued by police who were equipped with equally formidable weapons and had orders to shoot to kill, the Arabs stood paralyzed by the apparition of the one force that is stronger than the fear of death—the body of a lovely nude woman. They were rooted to the spot on which they stood, they had lost all instinct for self-preservation. They stood so for a while—and they would surely have been shot had not Madame Michele put two fingers in her mouth and produced a piercing sound, a warning whistle, and indicated to the Arabs the way out of the place.

The shouting of the police was heard outside and, stumbling over the masses of chairs and small tables, the Arabs fled in the direction of the washroom and escaped through a window there. Their life was spared by Gala, for the police entering the room, with their automatic guns held in front of them ready to fire, reacted to the nude exactly as had the Arabs. They became motionless, forgot their function, forgot the pursuit of the enemy, and lost their minds. Only when Monsieur Corti ordered Gala to cover herself and to get upstairs did the police get into motion and pick up where they had left off and start a thorough search of the place.

People came running into the Relaxez-Vous. The shooting, the agitation, the voices, the entry and escape of the Arabs, the morbid desire to see at close range a bloody tableau, to be part of the corrida, held everyone spellbound. The police made order by shouting, "Take your places, sit down, nobody leaves, remain as you are," and other official phrases. Some of the helmeted gendarmes, weapons cocked, rushed down the cellar door, others mounted the circular cast-iron stairway that wound up to the apartment of Miomo Corti. The Mother Superior, Monsieur Corti, Madame Michel, the taxidermist, Signor Vivanti, and a tourist had already seated themselves at a table. The tourist held a conservative gray business hat in one hand and in the other he had an expensive camera of German make. He was dressed in a somber suit, a plain white shirt, a conservative tie, and he had a gray overcoat folded on his lap. He looked at the Mother Superior, who was praying silently. The police started checking the people. They came to the tourist.

"Your papers."

The tourist handed his passport to the policeman.

A voice in the room asked: "Who is he?"

The policeman said: "An American."

There were mumblings and French gestures. "Ah, that then, an American," said another.

The police screamed: "Quiet!" and "Sit down!" "Quiet—taisez-vous. Sit down, everybody, remain where you are."

A gendarme descended the circular staircase, saying gallantly:

"Careful, careful, pay attention. One can break one's leg on these little steps."

He turned. His round police countenance was void of all martial expression. He was helpless with the face that men wear who are in love or in the presence of great female beauty. He was the servant cavalier; he neglected his armor and held up both of his hands.

"Come, come, advance mademoiselle, descend. I will catch you if you fall."

One of the golden slippers appeared out of the round opening in the ceiling, and then a lovely leg, some canary-dyed ostrich feathers on the hem of her negligee, more of the lovely leg, the knee, the thigh. In her sunflower brightness, the beautiful girl descended. The room said, "Ah, Gala," relieved and by way of greeting. Gala smiled and sat down close to Corti.

"I found her all alone upstairs," said the gendarme, "and scared to death."

"How long are we to remain here?" asked Corti standing up.

Signor Vivanti set his bulging eyes on Gala and left them there most of the time like a fisherman staring at the float on his line.

"Sit down," shouted the gallant gendarme at Corti. "You stay until you are told to go," and another added, "You stay until the Inspector gets here. Depositions must be taken."

"I have to get back to my shop," said the taxidermist. "I have something on the fire."

"So do I," complained Madame Bernard, who owned the laundry.

"Everybody sit down and be quiet," said the police.

The door opened again, the felt curtain sailed into the room, more rain came in, and two policemen, both supporting a man, entered. The people made room. The two policemen brought the man to a table and sat him on a chair. The man seemed about to lose consciousness, his head fell back, he was pale and bled from a wound at the side of his head. The tourist got up, and matter of factly took off his jacket. He looked at the wounded man and said:

"Somebody bring me water, and bandages if you have any, and some disinfectant."

A policeman went to get a first-aid kit from the commissariat. Gala brought a dish with water. The Mother Superior held the sick man's head. It was like a scene in a passion play. The tourist removed the man's coat, looked at his face, and pulled down his eyelids. The Mother Superior handed him a sponge with water.

The tourist said: "Somebody call a doctor." The Mother Superior looked at the sick man and said: "Good Lord, it's Professor Clayborn." A policeman explained how they had found him. He had been hit at the side of his head, over the right ear, that was where the bleeding came from. Flying glass most probably.

The first-aid kit, which looked like an old tool chest, arrived. The tourist opened it and took a look. "This looks more like a tire-repair kit," he said.

The Mother Superior smiled. "We are a hardy race. But anyway, look, here is some iodine and a few bandages." He started to clean the wound.

Madame Michel said: "Anything, anything at all for Professor Clay Clay. Just ask me."

"Get some more clean water, first of all, and maybe we could give him a drink, some brandy. It's nothing serious, it just looks messy," said the tourist and repeated: "But anyway, somebody call a doctor."

He cleaned the side of the Professor's face. When the iodine was applied, the patient said: "Ah, ah, ah."

"It's all right," said the tourist. "It won't hurt after the first time."

"The doctor will take care of you, Professor Clayborn," said the Mother Superior.

"Ah yes, merci, good Mother," breathed the sick man.

"Let's give him some brandy," said the tourist. Madame Michel went to the bar and came back with a bottle that had no label and was filled with spirits of a yellowish color. She poured a water glass half full.

"What's this?" asked the tourist.

Madame Michel took the dirty bottle and wiped it off with her blue apron, and said:

"Excuse the bottle, the outside of it, but smell what is inside." She pulled out the cork and held the bottle under the tourist's nose. The man's face brightened. She explained: "Eau de vie, called William, made from pears called sweet William. I have a brother, an odd fish who has a small farm near Honfleur in Calvados, where all the world distills apple cider. He makes this liqueur from pears, only enough for himself and a few friends, and when you smell it, and close your eyes, you can see the pear tree. Here, taste some of it." She poured some in a cloudy glass for the Mother Superior, and she tasted it.

"Ah yes," she said. "Indeed I can see the pear tree," and she poured a good glassful into the Professor. The tourist smelled the glass in appreciation.

"Give some to the doctor!" said the Mother Superior.

"Not quite a doctor, just almost one," answered the tourist. "I'm only a laboratory technician," he added. He had cleaned the side of the man's face. "It's a splinter of glass and there is nothing to get it out with. I need a pair of forceps."

"I have a pair upstairs," said Gala, "a pair of tweezers." She ran to get them.

"You said you were almost a doctor," said the Mother Superior.

"Yes, I am a technician," explained the tourist, "for the hospital, for the laboratory. I specialize in blood."

"How fortunate that you are here," said the Mother Superior. She was holding Professor Clayborn's head to have it bandaged. Now waiting for the tweezers everybody relaxed and leaned back. From the Mother Superior's large blue sleeves came strong, healthy arms. The tourist examined them and said: "Excuse me, but you've got beautiful veins—"

The Mother Superior withdrew her bare arms into the protective wide sleeves of her religious garment and she said, with a degree of coquetry:

"Well, thank you very much, sir, no one has told me that before."

The tourist said: "Don't mention it, I didn't mean anything. I only wanted to say that from a medical point of view you have very nice veins. That's where I always draw blood, at the inside of the elbow."

Signor Vivanti sat close to Monsieur Corti. He had difficulty expressing his sentiments about Gala.

"*Creatura divina,*" he said. "You are a lucky man."

"It takes just a little push," said Miomo Corti, "to make this place—"

A new explosion shook the place. After a while the tourist said:

"Some people are interested in women, I am interested in veins, especially because that's my work—the collection of blood specimens."

"Of course, of course," said the Mother Superior.

The tourist gave a new cotton pad to the Mother Superior and said:

"Here, you'd better hold that over the wound while we're waiting for the tweezers."

The Professor opened his eyes and looked up. He searched the room with his eyes, he looked everywhere, he turned his head to look in back of himself, over the shoulder of the Mother Superior. She held him like a wiggling baby and she said:

"Quiet, she will be back any minute, she will come back. She has gone to get something for you."

The Professor closed his eyes. Exhausted, he slumped back.

Miomo Corti got up. "It will take hours before she finds what she's looking for among all her junk. I'd better go and see."

"Remain where you are," commanded the policeman at the door, and the one who had played the gallant before started to climb the stairs.

"After all," said Corti loudly, "I am her husband." The Professor opened his eyes and looked at Corti with some resentment.

"Shut up and sit down," said the policeman to Corti; he was halfway up the circular cast-iron stairs.

7·

The Tourist

"Is it interesting, your work?" the taxidermist asked the tourist.

"Oh very," said the tourist.

"In France, when we say interesting we mean do you make good money out of it."

"Very good," said the tourist. "I make as much as a doctor, more than some. I have my own house, a car, and privileges. I even have a special license on my car like a doctor. I can park, anywhere, any time, like a doctor. I carry a little black bag, just like a doctor. I live on Joralemon Street, across the river from New York, with a beautiful view of the harbor."

"At last, there she comes," broke in Miomo Corti.

Gala descended as she had before, with the aid of the policeman; she carried the tweezers.

"Now this is going to hurt just a little," said the tourist to the Professor and he asked Miomo Corti to pour a little more of the brandy in the glass. He dipped the tweezers into it to sterilize them, and then gave the brandy to the Professor.

"Drink it down and now hold still for a second — steady now. There we are — "

He put the splinter on the table and asked for a bandage. The Professor looked at Gala while the bandage was slowly rolled around his head.

"You were telling us about where you live," the taxidermist prodded the tourist.

"I get up in the early hours, before dawn, when it is still night, that's when I start. It's still dark when I drive down from the Heights. All the bridges of Manhattan are like golden harps laid across the river. The tops of the buildings glow like jewels. Below in Manhattan the city is asleep, it's dark. The sky is dark blue and so is the city. There is nothing so beautiful in all the universe, it's the greatest city in the world. I am now driving across one of the bridges and the sun is like a slice of watermelon in back of me. It burns dark red, in the mirror of my car. Slowly it rises and it begins to cast the shadow of my car ahead of me on the bridge. There is little or no traffic, I am all alone with the rising sun on this immense bridge, but it's a safe place. A big ocean freighter passes under the bridge, the top of the mast of the ship has a light on it—it almost touches, and there are ferryboats and barges. Oh, it's beautiful."

The Professor had been looking at Gala. The tourist had stopped winding the bandage.

The Mother Superior said: "I would very much like to see that. I would like to make a voyage to New York and drive across those big bridges. It must be very exciting."

The tourist said: "That can easily be arranged. You just come. You can stay with us, my wife and I. We'd be glad to have you. You know, sometimes when I drive across one of the bridges I think how good it is that it came out this way. My parents had a delicatessen, and they slaved all their lives to make me a doctor. I tried hard but I didn't make it—I failed in the exams. But the medical profession pulled me. A laboratory technician was the next best thing, so I worked at that.

"Then we bought the small house. My wife and my son sleep upstairs, so I can leave quietly in the morning. Next thing you know I am at a bedside on Park Avenue or on Madison Avenue. You get into all kinds of homes, even the Waldorf-Astoria Hotel or the Plaza. You meet all kinds of people. I say, 'I've come to get your blood.' Most of them just laugh, but some blanch at the sight of a needle."

Gala was looking into the Professor's eyes, he into hers. She held his hand, he kissed hers. Monsieur Corti talked to Signor Vivanti.

"You don't have to say another word," said the Italian. "I am sold."

The tourist continued his story:

"You get all kinds of experiences that way. I've got to go to get the blood before they have their breakfast. Then I drive up to Lenox Hill Hospital with my bag full of specimens, and that's a wonderful place. The night shift is still on. They have student nurses there and they are just about the prettiest women in the world, and nice and tidy in their little white collars and white shoes and white-and-blue-striped uniforms. Well, they all know me by name, and they all smile. And then I start on the way back. It's early still. You know, the night people in New York have time to be nice. The cops wave at me, they know my car. I stop and talk to the guy that runs the newsstand, he's full of jokes, and he's smiling as he hands me the paper. Maybe I stop and buy a fish at the market and get some fresh bread. Oh, the night people of New York are wonderful, there's nobody like them in the whole world. They've got a little time for you and a good word." The tourist looked into the old first-aid kit and said: "No adhesive tape in here. Well, so we make a knot." He knotted the bandage.

The Professor looked at the tourist. He said: "You've made me homesick."

"Sam Levine is my name. Glad to meet you." The tourist offered his hand. "You're French?"

"No, I'm American. Jeb Clayborn. I envy you. I don't know the night people. I only know the day people in New York. I was never able to talk to them. I didn't understand them and I don't think they understood me."

The Professor held his hand out toward the tourist. "I don't know how to thank you."

"Oh, that's all right, I would have done it for anybody."

"I envy you, you are a useful man."

"Well, I am sure you are too."

"I try to be, but I'm not."

"Oh yes you are, very useful," said the Mother Superior. She turned to the tourist. "The Professor teaches American literature here at a lycée."

"Well, that's a good, useful thing," said the tourist admiringly. The Professor shook his head. He said:

"I was a complete failure, a waster of time. I thought I would bring them Thoreau, Emerson, Mark Twain—but all they care about these days is an evening of television." He got up and tried to navigate toward the washroom. "It's the wrong thing—it's a world that no longer exists, perhaps never existed."

"Steady there," said the tourist.

"He's so pale," said Gala.

"I'm always pale."

"Give him more brandy," said Miomo Corti, and filled the glass. The Professor took it quickly and emptied it.

"He's had enough," said the Mother Superior, reaching for the glass.

The Professor held onto it and smelled it. "Yes," he said, "you can see the pear trees and the landscape. There is justification for this."

"In what?"

"In distilling a good thing like that, in putting it in a bottle."

He addressed the room, as if it were his class. "Or in getting up in the middle of the night like Mr. Levine and collecting blood in Manhattan, or in washing shirts, as Madame Bernard does, or in having a tavern well run, in being useful.

"Even if you are in a hospital and not a doctor you do something. It's a hand holding a hand. You have a reason for existence."

Then he said: "I am not a policeman, not athletic, not a businessman, not a doctor. I am useless, in the way of myself and everybody else."

"Now stop it," said the Mother Superior. "You are a very nice, a very dear, very good man, and everybody loves and respects you."

"Yes, I don't drink or smoke —" He looked hopelessly at Gala and from her to Miomo Corti and then dropped his hands in a gesture of futility. "I don't even make anybody unhappy," he said.

"You are a teacher and that is a noble profession and you should be proud of yourself," said the Mother Superior.

"Ah yes, madame, French children are very well brought up, and my pupils listen to me politely. I have come to France, to this last asylum, this refuge of the spirit. I love France, but my pupils are bored."

"Well, he loves France, that's already something," said the taxidermist. "What about France do you love the most?"

"The color of the little radishes," said the Professor, looking at Gala, and then he asked for his coat, but just as he was about to collapse the Mother Superior caught him in her arms, the tourist took hold of his legs, and they placed him on a bench that stood against the wall. The taxidermist put a screen around him.

"Let him rest for a while," said the Mother Superior.

"He's lonesome," said the tourist.

"He needs someone to love," said Gala.

The laundress who worked for Madame Bernard came in and said that the gas had been shut off and her place was like an icebox, and she asked the police if she could stay.

Notre Dame sounded the bells for the Ave Maria.

"Sit down and be quiet," said a gendarme to the laundress. The curtain sailed in again. A street musician, thin and wet with rain, came in and warmed his hands at the stove. Then he took his guitar and began to strum and sing his one and only tune.

"Je suis le vagabond, le marchand de l'amour." The police listened.

The musician paused and the tourist said after the applause: "Just somebody see that a doctor gets here and looks after him. It's nothing serious but one never knows. How long does it take to get a doctor here, anyway? Why, in America, we'd have an ambulance on the spot and a doctor would have been here in a matter of minutes."

A voice said: "Of course, in America everything is wonderful. Why don't you go home, American?"

The tourist said: "Oh, I am trying to get home."

"What's keeping you?"

"I came here for my vacation and I'm on the list for my return ticket. I've only been here for two weeks and I can't get out quickly enough. I'm tired of being swindled."

The Mother Superior took his hand. She said:

"Dear sir, I will devote the rest of the time you are here to showing you Paris, to let you see the beauty of our city, to take you to places where no one will take advantage of you, and when you get home, you will tell as wonderful a story of Paris as you do of New York."

Miomo Corti said to Vivanti: "To round out the program, I am going to get an additional act tomorrow. There's an Arab girl, working in a cheap place in Pigalle. She does an act with a python. It's crude but she has talent. One would not think that a python would make an erotic accessory but it does. I suppose it goes back to Paradise, to Adam and Eve and the serpent with the apple."

"You don't need a python, you need not worry," said Vivanti, "not with her—" He looked at Gala and said again devoutly: "Creatura divina."

"How old is she? How did you find her?"

Corti said: "Oh the patience, the work, until all was harmonious and there was no awkward gesture. Intimate dérobement is a serious business, it's harder than painting or sculpture. In a city, in a country in which cheap sex accosts you from every vitrine, where the senses are not left tranquil one minute by the stimulus of eroticism, in photographs, perfumes, songs, statuary, and movies, in the night especially, when the competition goes to work in streets filled with gaudy joints and tiresome travesties—to maintain a decent place is hard."

A policeman said, looking at his watch: "Now then, Madame Michel, what about that coffee?"

"I'm sorry," she answered, "it's the gas, it's shut off. We'll have to try with the alcohol stove."

Corti turned toward the American tourist:

"You said that you had been swindled, monsieur, here in Paris?"

"Yes, right down there in a restaurant on place Saint something—"

Corti helped him: "Place St. Michel—yes—tell us—"

"I go in, I ask for a menu, I order the table d'hôte for twelve new francs. But it's too rich for me, too many dishes, so I say to the waiter, 'Bring me everything on this card, but not the fish,' and so he does. Then I ask for the bill. The charge for food is fifteen new francs, so I say, 'This must be a mistake, my friend, I ordered the twelve-new-franc menu, and you charge me fifteen, especially since I did not have the fish.' He calls the proprietor who says, 'Yes, the bill is in order, monsieur. You see, monsieur, the table d'hôte menu included the fish, but you did not have the table d'hôte menu, you did not take the fish, you ate à la carte, and that adds up to fifteen new francs.' So I had to pay."

The Mother Superior, who was sitting down at her old place next to Corti, said: "That is not nice at all, something like that to happen to a visitor to our country."

The taxidermist asked: "Why didn't you call the police?"

The laundress observed: "Ah poof, the police, what would that accomplish!" A general discussion about being swindled began everywhere. "Do you know what happened to me?" said one. "Those crooks at the Rose Rouge—" Another screamed: "The thieves out in Ville d'Avray. Imagine. I give a dinner at a place called Chez Tante Marie—" and so it went with everyone having a story to tell of how he was swindled. Madame Michel poured some drinks out of another cloudy bottle.

Monsieur Corti said to Vivanti: "She projects, she is ravishing, Gala is more beautiful than all the statuary and the paintings in the museums of Paris."

"You don't have to convince me, I am sold. I know how rare beauty is. There was only one Venus, there is only one—this is the one."

"Madame Michel," said Corti, "I am going to the Place Pigalle tomorrow night, to see about that act. Will you stay here with Gala?"

"I am sorry," said Madame Michel, "but I have promised my

wife and my son to be with them tomorrow night. The show opens the day after, and I won't have another chance."

"Allow me," said Vivanti to Corti. "Let me take her to dinner. I will make myself free tomorrow."

There was no way out and Corti nodded: "I warn you, it will be a dull evening. She has no brain, no more sex than a snail, and no humor."

Vivanti opened his lizard mouth, and shifted his eyes to Gala. He said he would call for her. She looked at her husband for final confirmation. "You may go," he said. He had thought better of Vivanti, who now turned out to be a typical man of affairs, of no conscience, no manners. There was nothing new under the sun, especially in the domain of sex.

The tourist turned to the Mother Superior and asked: "Did I hear right? Did Madame say that she was going to visit her wife?"

Madame Michel answered directly across the table, saying: "Yes, you heard right, monsieur, for I am a man. That is, I was until I decided to change my sex." From her bag Madame Michel took a billfold and took some photographs from it. One showed a soldier in uniform. "This shows me doing my military service in the last war. This here is my son Roger, who is a psychoanalyst. Thanks to God I have not had the need of his services, for I am perfectly well adjusted. And here, this permit"—she handed it to the Mother Superior to translate—"listen to what it says. It is issued by the metropolitan police of Paris and gives me the right to dress up as a woman and go about the city as such. And also to perform on the stage as a female impersonator."

"Yes, that is what it says," said the Mother Superior, and Miomo Corti added that France was a civilized country.

The door opened, rain blew in again. The Clochard, whom everybody greeted joyously as "King Dagobert," entered with Lily at his side and with the Inspector of Police.

"Now," said Corti to the tourist, "here is the proper guide to show you Paris—every fouled nook and stinking corner of it. Here is everything Parisian that Chevalier and Piaf have ever moaned about—a real clochard. Do you know what a clochard is, doctor? Well, you go around New York and collect blood. A clochard goes around Paris and picks up fleas and cigarette butts, old bottles, false teeth, and he's very proud, he calls himself a free man. But when it gets freezing cold like today, then he joins our despised society, he warms himself near our stove, reads our papers by our light, and is not above accepting a cigarette or a glass of wine."

Madame Michel said: "At last, the coffee is ready."

The Mother Superior said: "I'd love to have a cup of coffee for the Professor back there. He isn't at all well."

"I am sorry, good Mother," said Corti, "but it's all for the police."

"There's not a drop more, see for yourself," said Madame Michel.

She poured it. A policeman took the tray full of mugs and said to the Clochard: "Out of my way."

The Clochard did not move. He addressed the policeman: "You do not have even a single cup of coffee to spare for the good Mother Superior?"

The policeman said: "Get out of my way, King Dagobert."

"Go, Lily," said Dagobert, and the cold little girl fled to the arms of the Mother Superior.

The old man stood there, monumental in his ragged vestments—a carmine shawl, his faded coat, his battered bowler hat, and his hands in gloves with holes in them, his bearded face, and his white hair like a mane—he was all majesty and he had rosy cheeks and merry eyes.

In a curious uncertain motion as if a clown were starting out on a tightrope he came forward toward the policeman. He balanced himself for a moment on one foot, and then, bringing the other foot forward and up with all his might, delivered a kick which sent the tray with the mugs of coffee, into the air, creating a clatter and sending a brown fountain of coffee down over the policeman. There was a great deal of laughter and hand clapping. King Dagobert stood and looked embarrassed: "Excuse me," he said.

The reactions of a policeman to happenings outside his normal routine are not in the book of rules. A coffee bath is unusual. He shook himself like a wet poodle. Madame Michel wiped his face with a dish towel, and he cursed the Clochard with his usual string of dirty words, and shook his cape.

The Mother Superior got up and said to the Inspector: "Please, Jeannot, arrest him."

The tourist had his second great surprise of the evening.

He looked at the Mother Superior. "Did you ask to have him arrested?"

"Yes," answered the Mother Superior. "When it's cold like that, clochards can go to a public assistance shelter, to a hospice of the Salvation Army, or to a monastery. But they don't like the smell of charity, or of holy water for that matter. They prefer to go to jail, where they find their friends. It's their way of life and one must respect it."

The Inspector took the Clochard by the arm, and he turned to the policeman who had had the coffee thrown over him. "Maurice," he said, "arrest him. Lock him up."

"Where?" said the policeman. "The place is filled with Arabs."

"Take him to the Santé then."

"They don't want anybody there. They are full of generals."

"Alors," said the Inspector, "what is France coming to? We can't let him go free on a day like this, and kick him out in the cold, and he won't go to the monastery. He's a difficult one. He knows his rights. Well, take him over to the Palace of Justice — put him in the salad basket there for the night. See that he gets a mattress and a blanket."

The policeman saluted, and, taking his prisoner with him, left.

The Inspector announced that everybody could go home now.

Signor Vivanti insisted on saying good night to Gala.

They found her behind the screen. She and the Professor were sleeping peacefully like two children.

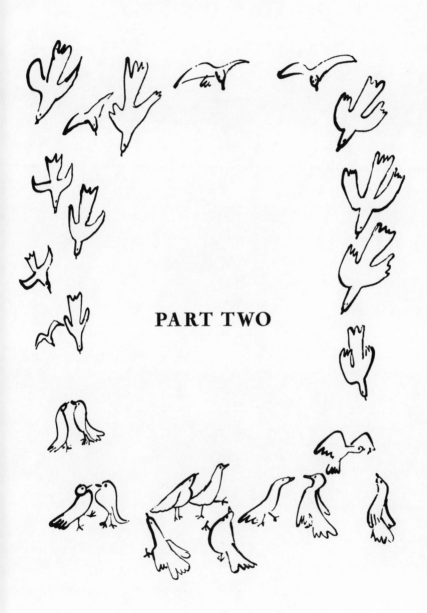

PART TWO

8.

The Tour d'Argent

AS IF OUT OF A TUNNEL, in a humid landscape, far away the bells of Notre Dame were ringing, ringing that melody which seems to say, "We will always be here, we will repeat it eternally."

The Cortis' bedroom faced upon a side street. It was papered in a faded tint of beige, the color of old cigars long exposed to the sun in store windows. A pattern of blue fleurs-de-lis was on this paper, which in places hung loose from the wall.

The one window was curtained with violet velvet drapery. On the ceiling were remnants of a stucco décor and from it hung a two-branch gas chandelier. A shaft of light cut through the room like a huge knife. It passed through a cage with two lovebirds, lighting them up green as glass and chattering; it went on through floating gray dust and reached back to a closet stuffed with Gala's many furs. On a dresser were jewels and gloves, and a stand held the intimate garments of both Monsieur and Madame Corti. The bed was held in place by a theatrical trunk used as a night table. The bed, in disorder as was the rest of the room, was filled with pillows and bolsters and out of it hung one small foot attached to the lovely left leg of Gala.

There was a soft knock on the door. Then the door opened and Madame Michel, dressed in her workaday outfit of blue jeans, a blouse, scarf, and slippers, came in carrying an immense basket of long-stemmed white roses and tall white branches of blossoming lilacs, all tied with a broad satin ribbon. A stuffed white dove with a card in its beak was attached to the high, looping, wickerwork handle of the basket. Madame Michel placed it near the window and silently left.

The telephone which stood on the trunk close to the bed rang. Next to the telephone was an ash tray. The phone kept ringing. Gala sat up, reached over, and picked up the instrument.

"Ah, it's you," she said. "Good morning." The voice talked rapidly. She said: "Speak a little lower." She smiled and said: "I too find you adorable."

Suddenly her head twisted involuntarily to her side, to the wall. Miomo Corti had risen in one quick motion, slapped her face, and gotten out of bed.

He was dressed in an elaborate bathrobe and pajamas. His

72

face was ashen, his eyes looked as if someone with a stylograph had worked endless circular lines around them. His gray hair was in disarray. He kicked the ash tray aside, kicked the phone to the floor, and walked around it looking at it as if it were a hostile creature about to jump up and strike at him. An agitated voice continued out of the phone, "'Allo—'Allo."

Corti bent down to it and shouted:

"I don't know who you are, monsieur, but you are impolite. You awaken us in the middle of the night. I find you disgusting!"

Gala was used to slapping and had no particular reaction to it. It brought color to her cheeks, she looked radiant. Her husband leaned down, picked up the phone, and put it back in its cradle.

"Who was it?" Corti yelled. "I want to know!" She pointed at the large basket of flowers and said: "Your friend, Vittorio Vivanti."

"Why didn't you say so, idiot!" said Corti. "Oh—oh—oh—you're driving me insane." He looked at the flowers and took the card. "You stayed out most of the night—you find him adorable—and he sends you an excessively expensive bouquet of flowers. Now then—explain! What happened?"

He came close, and it was her habit to tilt her head away from him when he did so in order to avoid his loose hand as much as possible.

"What happened?" he screamed, taking her by the shoulders.

"We went to the Tour d'Argent—"

"Of course. He has to show you off. Why couldn't he have taken you to some small place?"

"Well, with his big Rolls-Royce—"

"And?"

"There we ate."

"You left here at ten and you came home after four o'clock in the morning—you couldn't have eaten all this time! Where did you go after dinner? Where did you end up?"

"At his hotel."

"You went to his hotel—to his room? Like a common little whore to a bordel!" He slapped her again.

"But it was the Louis Quatorze."

"The Louis Quatorze, like every other hotel, is a bordel! Ah, no wonder he is grateful and sending you flowers. What did he say on the phone just now?"

"He said how nice it would be if we were in bed together now, and the waiter would be bringing breakfast. He wouldn't be lonesome."

"Were you in bed with him?"

"No."

"The ugly toad. And you said that you found him adorable—"

"Well, he said that he found me adorable as a woman. I was only being polite to him."

Corti moved back and forth at a trot.

"Oh, this is awful! Tell me the truth, don't lie, swear to me— did you go to bed with him?"

"But of course not!"

"I must know—I must be sure—look at me—do you swear?"

"I swear, of course I swear—"

He pulled back the curtain, the light streamed in, she sat in bed; he kneeled on the bed, pulled back her hair, and took her head in his hands; he bent it back and looked at her close.

"Look at me—look into my eyes!"

She did.

"Yes," he said, "I believe you. The eyes don't lie. Oh that dirty old lecher! You poor innocent child! Just the same, everybody at the Tour d'Argent, and in that hotel every clerk, telephone operator, room waiter, and maid takes it for granted that you slept with him, that you are his little whore. Don't laugh, it's terrible. You are so beautiful, so pure, so innocent, and so stupid!"

He sat down on the bed dejectedly.

"The old swine. I am sure he tried everything to make you sleep with him. You don't have to tell me, I know. What happened from the moment you left here? I must know everything. You went to the Tour d'Argent where, of course, Signor Vivanti was greeted by everyone from the owner down, and properly taken care of. Go on from there."

"Well, they all know him there—"

"Important client—'Bon soir, Your Excellency.'"

"He ordered first, from a beautiful, big menu, and the proprietor himself came to take the order."

"Naturally. Signor Vittorio Vivanti is a very important man."

"We had the best table in the room, overlooking Notre Dame and the Seine, and the Cathedral was lit up, and then he said how beautiful it was and how even more beautiful it would be if I went to bed with him after dinner."

"Impossible—the swine—at the start—just like that. What did you say?"

"I said nothing."

"You were shocked."

"No. I was reading the menu because it was the first time I

was at the Tour d'Argent and because it was all so beautiful and the first time I could order what I wanted to eat. That is, Signor Vivanti did the ordering. I never had such a meal. Let me tell you what he ordered: first caviar, as much as I wanted, with little pancakes and champagne, and then—"

"Spare me the food. Tell me what he said."

"He talked about going to bed—"

"With the caviar?"

"Yes. He said that was very good for it. He said it several times while they were bringing the caviar and he told me to eat all I wanted. He ate a mountain of it. Then came a lovely soup Germiny à l'oseille, and the next course was wonderful, a sole in a white wine sauce, with truffles, mushrooms, and little moon-shaped bits of pastry."

"And what did he say?"

"He said he was very lonesome in his big suite at the Louis Quatorze."

"And did it never occur to you to say to this man, 'Monsieur! unless you change this conversation immediately, I will get up and leave you!'"

"Well, he is much older than I am and you asked me to be nice to him. He wanted me to call him 'tu' but I addressed him as 'vous' and 'Monsieur Vivanti' throughout."

"Go on, tell me what he said."

"I had finished eating the fish and then came the owner of the restaurant again and he took me out on the balcony and showed me the scenery and the ship below that was lit up and had just turned around—the bateau mouche filled with tourists. The owner of the restaurant asked how everything was, and Monsieur Vivanti said that it was all excellent."

"So then?"

"So then we went back to the table. They had cleared away everything."

"What did he say?"

"Monsieur Vivanti asked me to come home to his hotel with him, after dinner."

"Preposterous; the mentality of this man, to take a young married woman out, the first time, and to ask her at dinner to go to bed with him. To ask anyone that at any time is in the worst bad taste, but at dinner it is awful. But go on. What happened next?"

"Next came the pressed duck. That was the best, and the Tour d'Argent, Monsieur Vivanti explained to me, was the best place in the world to have pressed duck, and we got a card with the number of the duck on it. The duck was presented on a silver platter, it was brown as toast, and then it was taken away, and Miomo it's like in church during High Mass, in Notre Dame near the High Altar. There were three fat headwaiters like cardinals, with napkins stuck in their necks. Each one stood in a niche, like in a tabernacle with a light shining down on him, and each one had a duck in front of him, and silverware, and sauce boats, and they sharpened knives, and then they cut up the ducks, that's all they do all night long, and then it's put, that is the carcass of the duck is put into silver presses, and they twist and turn a handle and then the blood comes out of a spigot—"

"Will you stop talking about food and come to the point. Vivanti—what about him—what did he say?"

"He said how wonderful it was and how glad he was I enjoyed it all and he said how he would enjoy to go to bed with me—"

"And then?"

"And then came the duck and they served the red wine with it. This was even better than the fish."

"And you just kept on eating, you didn't ever answer him?"

"Well, I said that it was the most wonderful meal I had ever had."

"So what did he say?"

"Well, the same thing."

"So what did you say?"

"I said nothing."

"So what did he say?"

"He said he was very hurt and he wanted to know why I didn't want to go to bed with him. I said, 'I'm sorry, but I can't jump in bed with anyone just because he wants it.'"

"So?"

"They had wonderful soufflé potatoes with the duck. You know, not those you get in other restaurants that are like parchment, or potato chips. These were soft and then there was that wonderful sauce."

"What about Vivanti? What did he say?"

"Just then he couldn't say anything, because the proprietor was back at the table and asked how everything was, and the wine waiter asked how it tasted, and the headwaiter, so Signor Vivanti didn't say anything except 'fine, fine, fine, excellent—very good, thank you.'"

"How discreet."

"It tasted wonderful. He ate and drank and then he wiped some of the fat and sauce off the plate with bread, and ate it, and then he wiped his mouth."

"How vulgar, and you sitting there with him! So what did he

say by way of answer when you told him you couldn't jump in bed with just anyone?"

"Yes, he wiped his mouth and took a swallow of wine and then he said that he wasn't 'just anyone —'"

"Oh yes, we know that. Go on."

"He picked his teeth, but very elegantly in back of a napkin that he held in front."

"How chic. Continue!"

"He looked very sad, and ordered some dessert. What would I like, he asked me, and then he told the headwaiter that we would both like some crêpes suzette. He asked me if I liked that and I said yes, of course, very much. I'd like anything he ordered."

"Except a bed!"

"I will never forget this dinner as long as I live."

"I am sure you never will."

"It was the best meal of my whole life."

"So then?"

"They cleared the table."

"Oh yes, and the discreet seducer from Milano sat silent, perhaps with his hand on your leg, looking down your décolleté."

"No, he was very proper, I must say."

"Oh, the very model of an Italian gentleman. What did he say?"

"He said he was surprised."

"At what?"

"That I was so narrow-minded and did not want to go to bed with him. I said, 'You know, Monsieur Vivanti, the fact that I parade myself naked on the stage doesn't mean that I sleep with everybody who asks me!' I said that furthermore I was a respectably married woman and loved my husband."

"Did you really say that?"

"Of course. I can't make up things like that, it's the truth."

"So how did he react to that?"

"'Of course,' he said. He knew and he had great regard for you."

"One never knows one's true friends. Go on. What happened next?"

"So now they made the crêpes suzette. All at the table on silver platters and everything done by hand in front of us, scraping the orange peel, and the lemon peel, and mixing the butter with orange juice and the liqueurs—"

"Now the waiters and the proprietor were around you again."

"Well, he asked me how I came to meet you, and how I got into this business of which I am part, and about my beauty and how I got into this flea circus."

"Flea circus? What flea circus?"

"The Relaxez-Vous." Corti slapped her.

"Did you answer him? To that at least?"

"No, I said simply that it was my profession, because I had not learned anything else, and that I owed it all to you."

"So he said?"

"'Well,' he said, 'well, my darling, carissima, soon you won't have to do it any more,' and then he asked me again to sleep with him."

"Good Lord, it's like listening to a train going over rails, or to an ode by Klopstock."

"What is that?"

"You wouldn't know. It's a German poet I tried reading to stay awake for your return, Gala, all through the night. I fell asleep with it. What about Signor Vivanti?"

"So he painted a picture for me of all he would do for me, the life he would give me if I became his friend."

"That mangy dog, all that the first time he goes out with you. I should have never let you go. Then?"

"Then he asked me if I wanted more crêpes suzette, and I said yes."

"How could you eat, with this talk going on?"

"Oh, it goes in one ear and out the other."

"What happened next?"

"I said to him, 'I am sorry but I cannot leave Miomo. He is my husband, and he has taught me all I know. My life is to dance, to do my act on the stage.'"

"What did he say to that?"

"Nothing, the waiter came and said, 'Will monsieur have any more crêpes? Will madame have any more?' So I ate more, and I ate his too. 'Anyway,' he said, that is Signor Vivanti said, 'I will make a great actress of you, a star,' and would I sleep with him after. He asked for a cigar and lit it, and for some brandy, and then he started again, looking at me with his bulging eyes, like a frog and repeating, quack, quack, 'sleep with me.'"

"And you? What did you say?"

"Oh Miomo, I got a feeling of sickness, I didn't want to listen any more, I got lonesome for this place, for my little stable downstairs. He looked at me again and I said, 'Please don't ask me any more, please arrest this conversation. I cannot listen to any more of this talk, I will get sick and you will have to take me home right away.'"

"At last—and of course there was nothing more to eat. What did he say?"

"'Finish your crêpes suzette,' he said, and he told the waiter to give me some more champagne. But he was quiet for a second and then he asked me why I didn't want to go to bed with him, when every other girl did. He said that he had stayed an extra day in Paris, just to see the act, and to take me out and have dinner with me, and to make plans and that I owed it to him to sleep with him."

"How disgusting! But go on!"

"He said that he could have had dinner with another girl, and then slept with her and had no problems. So I said that I was very sorry, but that he should have taken that other girl and why did he insist on taking me? So he said, because he loved me. I said, 'You come to Paris for a day, you see me, you say you fall in love with me. That isn't love, love is for long years, love is forever.' So he looked very sad and then he sighed and asked for the check. 'I loved you the moment I saw you,' he said. 'Haven't you ever heard of love at first sight?'"

"How romantic. Go on."

"I can't stand anybody looking sad, so I said, 'Monsieur Vivanti, I am sorry. You know it's much easier to say yes to a man than to say no. But I can't go to bed with you, or anyone else. I am full of complexes about going to bed with people, or about taking my clothes off. In fact I couldn't do it, and have never done it except in public.'"

"What did he say to that?"

"He said, 'Try it with me, it will make no difference to our friendship, nobody will know about it, and I will respect you as before.'

"So I said, 'Please let's talk about something else. Look at the beautiful view.' He called for the check again. The waiter came with the check. Signor Vivanti never looked at it, he didn't add it up. He reached in his pocket and took out a pack of big bills as if they were lottery tickets, and he covered the check with them and pushed it away. Then he gave one to the headwaiter. Then he snapped his fingers and gave another one to the wine waiter, and then they all bowed and pulled chairs, and he went down the elevator and he gave another bill to the doorman and then we got into his big Rolls-Royce and he started again. He said, 'We'll drive to my hotel.' He took my hands and asked me again to sleep with him.

"I said, 'If you had met me at someone's home, or anywhere except at the Relaxez-Vous, would you allow yourself to talk to me this way?'

"So he said that he talked to all women the same way. I asked if he talked to his wife like that also.

"He said, 'No, not to my wife.'

"I said, 'Why not?'

"He said, 'Because she is my wife!' Then he said it was early and did I want to go to see a cabaret, so we went to Monseigneur and that was very nice. And then I had an idea. I wanted to go back to the Indifferent."

Miomo Corti jumped up. "Oh God no, why did you want to do a thing like that for? To go back to that place."

"I just wanted to see the show, to see the girls there."

"So they all know! You go there with this monstrous creature! Did you tell him that you had worked there?"

"Yes, of course. Besides he bought champagne for everybody, and the Rolls was waiting outside with the chauffeur—very chic, everybody admired it."

"Was the place full?"

"Not at first, but then word got around, and they all came—from the street, from the Sphinx, the Semiramis, the New Paradise. It suddenly was packed and people stood three deep at the bar."

"So what did he say?"

"He couldn't talk about going to bed because everybody sat with us, and the owner of the club said that any time I wanted to come back I would be welcomed with open arms. I had been the greatest attraction since they opened."

"It's getting pretty late now. When did you go to his hotel?"

"Yes, he too said that it was getting late and he would take me to his hotel and that there he had a beautiful apartment with a fine view of Paris."

"What happened next?"

"We were ready to go when the proprietor of the Indifferent said that there was great ambiance, and everybody asked me to do one of my numbers."

"Good Lord! The final degradation!"

"So because after all I had to do something for Signor Vivanti and because everybody begged me, the musicians, the girls, and because the director took me by the hand, and introduced me to the audience, so suddenly I was there on the stage, and I did 'Tourbillon.' And then there was such applause that I did 'Profound Mirror,' and as an encore 'Les Plaisirs Clandestins.'"

Monsieur Corti held his head in both hands. He cried: "But

have you gone altogether crazy? Especially 'Les Plaisirs,' my latest creation, and not to be shown around—at the Indifferent!" He slapped her three times.

"Well, I thought you wouldn't mind. I only sort of tried it out. Besides it was announced that it would be part of the new show at the Relaxez-Vous, and he gave you credit and also the address."

"How did it go?"

"They went hysterical, but I did not give another encore."

"And the old swine was now excited and wanted to get to bed immediately."

"He said that I was a great artiste."

"Then you went to the hotel?"

"Yes, then we went to the hotel."

"Up to his room! Oh, this is unbearable but go on."

"He was very nice."

"You went—just like that?"

"No. I didn't want to go up at first. I said, 'It's late, please let me go home, I can take a taxi,' but he said, 'Just come up for a moment.'"

"So you are in his room. Go on."

"He showed me the view, he asked me again to please call him Vittorio. Then he asked me to go to bed with him. I said, 'Look, you can call up your other girls, or call the Indifferent. They will send you somebody, anybody you want, but I can't go to bed with you.'"

"What did he say?"

"He said, 'Why not?'"

"I said, 'It's impossible because of my husband' and there

suddenly I had to burst out laughing, for I was thinking of you, so Signor Vivanti also laughed, and he asked me what I was laughing at, and I told him how funny it was."

"And he said?"

"He said, 'All women are crazy. Here you refuse my love, and you laugh at your husband. What kind of a brain have women got?'

"I said, 'I had to laugh because it was all so sad.'

"He said, 'Oh, I thought you laughed because you had changed your mind, one never knows with women. I don't understand them, and the older I get, the less I understand them.' I said that I was sorry.

"He said, 'You have ruined my whole evening for me. There is so little in this life to remember with any pleasure, and it is over so quickly.'"

"One must say, he has persistence."

"So he said, 'Explain to me why you won't go to bed with me. Here you are in my room, nobody will know.'

"I said, 'But I have explained it to you. I told you that I could go to bed only with somebody I loved.'

"'Love,' he said, 'what is love?'

"I said, 'Love is when you walk hand in hand in the street, and you see nobody else and it has nothing to do with bed.'

"So he asked if I walked hand in hand with you down the street and saw nothing else.

"So I said, 'Well, I did once.'

"So he said that if it had nothing to do with bed, why not do it?

"But I did not answer. He asked if there was anything I wanted.

"I said yes, that I was very hungry, I wanted something to eat.

"So he said that he was hungry too, but that the room service at the Louis Quatorze was terrible and everything took hours and came up cold even during the day.

"So he said that he knew a place that was still open, a small place, and there we went, and they had something wonderful, a veritable grand specialité of the house, le jambon Arcadie, a ham, so light it seems to float on a bed of spinach au gratin—I never ate anything like it—with some mushrooms in cream around it and an Italian dessert with wine."

"So what did he say?"

"I asked him if, because I did not go to bed with him, it was all over, and if any actress or artiste who did not go to bed with the producers, directors, or owners of theaters would be finished.

"'It has nothing to do with it,' he said. 'Talent is so rare, beauty is so rare—'

"He took my hand, and he said, 'No matter with whom you slept if you have no talent, you will not get there,' and not to worry, he would see to it that I became a star, he would help me because I had beauty and talent."

"Tiens, tiens, so he finally gave up."

"He told me that he had to go to Milano by plane today and then he would come back and give a big party at the Relaxez-Vous. I was so sleepy. In the car he said, 'I will be very grateful, always, I will love you always.' He kissed me."

"Of course. Like a father."

"Yes, like a father."

"So what did he say next?"

"He said, 'When do I see you again?'

"I said, 'You are a very important man, Monsieur Vivanti, and as you say all the girls want to sleep in your bed, so don't waste another evening on me.' He leaned back in his corner of the car and he said, 'Such a thing has never happened to me before.'

"So we were again in front of the hotel, and he held me by the arm.

"He said again, 'Come up just for a moment.'

"But I said, 'I have seen the view from your lovely apartment and I thank you for a wonderful evening, but I am dead of fatigue. Please let me go.' But he said, 'Just a minute. Come up just for a minute. I have a surprise for you.' So I said, 'But you promise!'

"'Yes,' he said, 'I promise. I have a present for you. Just come for a minute,' and we went up the elevator."

"Bon Dieu, is this never coming to an end?"

"He wanted to give me something."

"So you go to his room a second time. What happens now?"

"When we were there he opened a bottle of champagne and then he turned on the television, but there wasn't any. The Eiffel Tower was all violet in the morning light. He picked up some telegrams; he said it would be wonderful if I were as crazy about him as he was about me. Then he said I would lose all my friends if I behaved with them as I did with him."

"Touching, his concern for me."

"Then he asked me to go to bed with him, for the last time. I shook my head. Then he said that most probably I wasn't any good in bed anyway, and I said I was certain I wouldn't be. So he said he wanted to get a little sleep, his plane was leaving early, and he said his chauffeur would take me home."

"And what did he give you?"

"He forgot to give it to me."

"I said good night and that I was sorry for having ruined his evening. He said maybe it was better so, but he looked very tired. He started to put things away in his suitcase, put some papers into folders, and he looked around for things to put in his pockets and it all made me feel terrible. Then he took me down and put me in his car and told his chauffeur to take me home. I sat in the car alone and I had to cry because life is so sad. 'I will call you tomorrow morning and give Miomo my best,' he said.

"I said, 'Forgive me.'

"He said, 'Of course,' so the car drove on. At the Place de l'Alma, the chauffeur stopped the car and he said, 'Madame, excuse me, but may I ask you a great favor?'"

"No, not the chauffeur also!"

"So I said, 'What is it?'

"He said, 'I am a married man. My wife is insanely jealous and she poisons my life. She does not believe that every night Signor Vivanti rolls from one place to the other, all night long, from one restaurant to another, from Maxim's to the Tour d'Argent to the Elephant Blanc, to the Left Bank, to the Right Bank, to night clubs, to parties, to private houses until four or five in the morning. She thinks I am out with other women, and so tonight I put her into the baggage trunk of the car, and took her along, so that she finds out for herself, and now I would like to let her out, if you don't mind.'

"So I said, 'Of course, let her out immediately.'

"So he opened the trunk of the car, and his little wife came out and stretched herself, and she thanked me, and sat in front with him, and she put her arms around his neck while he was driving, and she said that she forgave him. And that is all."

As she talked Gala was busy feeding her two small birds who cracked sunflower seeds with their parrot jaws. Outside in the street the crash of little boys' voices was heard as they came rushing out of school. Gala stood against the sun-lighted window, her lithe figure silhouetted, and Miomo Corti studied her. He said:

"I too forgive you, Gala." But she did not hear it. There was the sound of the bells for the full midday concert from the towers of Notre Dame.

9.

Turn Over, Please

TWICE A WEEK there came to the Relaxez-Vous an apostle-like figure, an herb and cereal eater with hair hanging down to his shoulders and also growing out of his ears and nostrils, a bearded naturopath, amateur yogi, advanced in years but of rustic hardiness. He managed, small as he was, to give the impression of larger stature, especially when he inhaled and exhaled. His eyes had the hypnotic beam of the possessed. He was armed with hands like wrenches and made his living with them, being a registered and licensed masseur.

He was dressed as one living in a deep forest, in the protective colors of scouts and hunters, in field grays and greens, loden cape, and taupe-colored sweater. He smelled like a haystack, and over his shoulder he carried a kind of haversack, bought at an army surplus store on the Place de la Bastille, a one-time motorcycle dispatch rider's canvas bag that had U. S. lettered on it and had seen bitter service. It had a webbed shoulder strap and was testimony to the quality of the materials that go into American army goods; it was indestructible.

It contained some baby powder, rubbing alcohol, and the various health foods from which Herr Doktor Ueberlinger, as he was called and titled by Miomo Corti, drew his strength.

He brought his own towel; he also was more reliable than the official weather forecast, functioning by closeness to the universe.

Light of step, whipping along in monk's sandals, his feet bare in summer and in winter in hoary socks, his approach was swift and sure; he was always on time. Gala waited for him like a trapped bird.

He came twice a week to refresh himself at the sight of the wonder of the human body, to labor to retain the youthful tensility, to banish every trace of cellulity from the lovely thighs and the rounded knees. With hands that were like pumice stones he snatched, beat, pulled at the young woman's body.

There were four wooden blocks in the Corti apartment, and with Corti and Madame Michel helping, the Doktor lifted the bed on these to bring it up to the proper height so that he could work on his patient. He was under strict surveillance during the time of troweling and slapping, and the cries for help of the wretched damsel in her ghastly hour-long going over.

Miomo Corti always sat on guard. He would read *France-Soir,* the funnies first, and after that he would search for items of particular interest, which he would then read aloud. Knowing the routine of Herr Doktor Ueberlinger thoroughly, he would lower his paper and stop reading when the masseur, sweating freely, approached the tender alabaster hills, the beautifully formed bosoms on which a strict hands-off policy was in force. "Turn over, please," the Doktor would say when he had belabored all there was accessible to his kneading at the front.

This would be an especially thorough going over, for while the Doktor hung up his haversack and took off his outer garments, his gloves, and then arranged the baby powder and the bottle of alcohol, Miomo Corti told him about the night with caviar, sole Marguery, duck and ham, and crêpes suzette. The Doktor shot punishing looks at Gala.

"She stuffed herself like a goose for Christmas," said Corti.

"So how do you feel after last night?" asked Doktor Ueberlinger, and answered himself: "Schrecklich."

"Poor girl," said Madame Michel, "she was half starved—she was hungry—she gets hardly anything to eat."

The Herr Doktor washed his hands. To protect the patient from a draft, he closed the windows.

Miomo Corti sat down at the foot of the bed and began to read *France-Soir* while Herr Doktor Ueberlinger sprinkled baby powder on the beautiful body.

"So, you made a pig of yourself," he said, showing his teeth which were yellow and oversized like the keys of an old piano.

He liked rhythm while he worked. He turned Gala's small radio to luncheon music. It was at one P.M. that he started, and now he turned up his sleeves and was ready to give himself up to his work.

The body was arranged. Doktor Ueberlinger, in correct, professional procedure, covered that part of the body which was not being massaged with a bedsheet and a towel.

"Relaxez-vous," he said in his heavy German accent and pressed down on her as if with two sandbags. He started with pressure here and there, and then came rhythmic strokes of varying intensity and depth, to the limits of tolerance to make the blood flow and to cause lymphatic flow.

The poor girl whimpered and Miomo Corti commanded her to be silent.

He began reading "Cheri Bibi," his favorite comic strip.

The Doktor worked to some music of Khatchaturian, which is ideal for tapotement, administered in quick, sharp blows, with the edge of the hands, and also with the hand used to cup, to slap, to pinch.

"That will get rid of that excess fat and ward off cellulity," he said. Cellulity was one of the most often-used warnings of the Doktor. He searched Gala's body thoroughly for traces of it.

"This appears in women mostly at the back of the upper leg, below the gluteal area." At the approach to which with either tapotement or fleurissage the poor girl tensed in a reflex contraction of the glutei, and the Doktor was again compelled to say, "Relaxez-vous."

The tuberosity, the bony protuberance of the pelvis, the cavity that receives the head of the femur, the inferior part of the hip, was treated with fleurissage, a kind of finger painting. His hands explored for flaccid tissue, searched for tightnesses, for deposits of fat, for bumpiness. The legs now being covered, he worked upward, to the muscles of the back, where he used all of his many methods, including knuckling and a kind of corkscrew twist, pinching on the gluteus maximus muscles, which in vulgar language are the muscles forming the backside and whose condition was one that caused anxiety to both the Doktor and Miomo Corti, for these, together with the gluteus medius, are the most fragile properties of beauty, and when sagging, or losing their contour, must be beaten back into perfect shape. They were rosy now, like raw pork chops, and the Doktor moved up to pattern the small of the back. Gala had buried her head in the pillow to stifle her agony, for she knew that outcries only made it worse. The Doktor moved up and down along the spine, up to the trapezius muscles. He used pressure, rolling, knuckling. He pulled the head to this side and that. He was sweating freely now; he wiped his forehead, and then commanded Gala to turn over.

"Curious case," said Corti, "the murder case in Ville d'Avray! This famous surgeon now — " He put down the paper to see that in the process of turning her over, the amenities were observed. The Doktor covered Gala, letting the sheet gently settle on her, then moving it up, so that only the right leg was bare. He sat down and took the foot in his hand, starting to work on the small toe.

"I am listening," said Herr Doktor Ueberlinger. "Go on with the Crime of Passion."

"You can call it that," said Miomo Corti. "I call it the Crime of Stupidity." He turned and held up the paper so Doktor Ueberlinger could see the picture of the accused.

"Look at that head of a pig, I don't think it will fit into the guillotine."

"Just the same the guillotine he will certainly get," said

Doktor Ueberlinger, strangling his way down along Gala's neck, "and richly deserve for his idiocy."

"The procurator general calls him a bad genie and asks for his head."

The Doktor was going through Gala's intestines, grappling with his thick fingers. She cried out.

"And the defense?"

"Oh, that then—listen to this. They called a character witness, who said that he could never have arrived at thinking that the good surgeon was an assassin. Everyone in the neighborhood esteemed him highly, he was known as a homebody, he helped his wife wash the dishes. His mother says that as a boy he was always obedient, and in an effort to save his life, states that as a small child he was retarded, sad, skinny with his large head and large nose and evasive look, at nineteen years of age he still read comic books, and he amused himself with a toy, a mechanical tractor which he was given when he was twelve. He was born prematurely."

"The younger he gets, the more innocent."

"A strange boy so thin he was known as 'The Plank' by the other boys, but somehow he became a surgeon, and somehow he became an honored citizen, mayor of the community, and owner of property—a married man."

"And a murderer!"

Gala cried out.

"Quiet," said Miomo Corti. "In the summing up—nothing new. On the table in front of the judges, a brutal instrument, a butcher knife."

"Very clever. So that the surgeon would never be suspected of operating with anything so awkward."

"He gets his mistress to murder his wife, under promise of marrying her, and then he delivers the mistress to the police and so is rid of both of them. For he has his attention fixed on a new one, seventeen years old. For one so retarded, *not* bad. Besides he has good taste. Take a look at the three women. Each one is exciting."

"Above all, the little one," said the Herr Doktor, now busy with Gala's thighs.

"Here is a new development," Miomo held up the paper to show the plan of the house. "Here in the mansarde lived the mother. On the first floor was the bedroom of the surgeon and his wife, and below them was the room in which the mistress lived. He had prepared it all carefully; he had given sleeping pills to his wife and when they had taken effect he tapped on the floor with his cane, the signal for the mistress to come up. He then took his wife, held her up in bed, and said, according to the mistress, 'Here, you imbecile,' indicating where to stab; he pointed where the heart was. Here she stabbed and the wife was dead."

"Oh God!" screamed Gala, "Please!" under the hands of the Doktor who was kneading her upper leg.

"So the surgeon washes his hands and goes to his favorite bistro, as he does every evening, and drinks sherry, seven of them, and at ten strokes of the rustic village church bell he returns home, and he discovers his dead wife and calls the police! His mistress, the poor fool who did it for love of him, who is still in love with him, who will go to the guillotine also of love for him, is arrested."

"Only a woman in love can be so stupid," said the Herr Doktor, and Gala paid for the stupidity of the mistress and her love for the doctor by getting several extra knuckles, pé-trissages, and combination tapotements and cupping on her abdomen.

The Doktor wiped the sweat from his forehead again.

"Perhaps this is why women do not go to the guillotine," he said. "Not for a crime passionnel because they are blinded by love."

"What will she get?"

"Seven years."

"Ah, here is the most profound observation of the trial. The mother of the accused says that it was all the wife's fault. The marriage was a failure because the wife did not prepare the little special dishes that her son, the surgeon, was so fond of."

The Herr Doktor rinsed his hands, dried them, and gave Gala a cleaning with rubbing alcohol.

"Well, that is that," he said.

Gala was covered with the sheet and a blanket.

Miomo Corti folded his paper. Gala lay as a body in the morgue, unconscious from exhaustion. Doktor Ueberlinger opened the windows for an airing, which the room was badly in need of. He collected his things and dressed himself and then, in his lightfooted fashion with the canvas dispatch case, he ran on his heavy-soled monk's sandals, a long distance, all the way up to his home.

10.

Aisha and Ali

THE NIGHT WHEN Gala went to the Tour d'Argent with Signor Vivanti, Miomo Corti had gone with the Commissaire de Brigade Mondaine to the lowest part of Paris, to the Arab quarter, the terrain of misery, off the Boulevard de Rochechouart. Here are the streets where the cheapest traffic in women took place.

The streetwalkers of Paris work mostly for Arabs and Corsicans. They are bought and sold like cattle. The pimps for whom they work have their clubs and meeting places here. It is the busiest milieu. The worst of these streets, the ones in which the poorest of the Arabs live, were now blocked off by police trucks. Gendarmes, heavily armed and in pairs, patrolled and kept the Arabs in their quarters. Here there had been a cabaret, and in it a girl named Aisha; she had been brought into the country from the native quarter of Algiers, from the place where no records of birth, death, disease, or murder are kept. She had a python with which she had performed a dance to cymbals, the whine of a reed instrument, and a small drum beaten with the flat hand. The Commissaire, a Corsican also, by name of Bontempi, had seen her and told Corti that he thought that there were possibilities.

"The eyes of that girl Aisha, they're not black, I mean just black; they are green-black, like foliage reflected in a pond, shadowy. They are at times, in the night, as if she were blind. But they see penetratingly."

"You are interested in her?" asked Miomo Corti with a trace of possessiveness.

"Well, in a way. Look, I am a police official, and besides a family man. She's a nice girl, you can trust her, she's clean."

"You mean morally—or bodily?"

"Both," said the severe representative of the Commissariat de Brigade Mondaine. "Now don't expect the impossible. Judge for yourself when you see her.

"She has large black eyes with gray rims, like a beautiful cat. These eyes, like those of most Africans, sometimes seem opaque, a dark kind of mother-of-pearl, and at other times they are flashing. All the woman lies in these eyes, her passion, her love, her docility, her mystery.

"She is like a beautiful cat, she moves like one, she has a transparent skin, her hair is black, black, her bust I would say is like Gala's, perhaps a little larger, her waist narrower, she has the most sexy, beautiful legs. She's primitive with a passionate physique. It's like a tiger walking around loose."

"You seem to know her well."

"The cabaret was under my surveillance. It is gutted now. It was a place called Scheherazade—there are a dozen by that name in Paris. In this street there was a night club in almost every house, with drumbeat, reedy music, and Arabian décor, lonesome places, souks, brass taborets, and a belly dancer. This one was the only one that had any allure.

"We'll have to climb. She takes sun baths, that is, the snake likes the sun, and they are all the way up near the skylight." The Commissaire thought that she could be bought and trained.

They found her in a room sitting on the floor. The snake was wrapped in a blanket and the girl answered to questions with open mouth, saying, "Ah?"—meaning that she wanted to have the question repeated.

She was half starved and dirty and the python also had had nothing to eat. She said that she took the animal to houses around the quarter to let him hunt for rats and mice, but the rodent population of Paris was as desperately trying to hold onto life as were the humans, no matter what the conditions. Slithering up and down and waiting in dark hallways and corners for hours, the results bore no relationship to the effort and patience of the snake. Ali remained hungry, and when he caught something it was scrubby game and showed on him like a swallowed ping-pong ball. So Ali dreamed of a better life and clung to Aisha for warmth.

When the girl obediently took her clothes off at the Commissaire's command, a curious body came out of her rags; her ribs showed, her bosoms, like those of most young Arabian girls, were well developed. She had heavy upper legs, and long thin feet. The Arabian skin was on account of dirt duskier than it normally is. She had masses of black hair, and although this personage by the standards of Miomo Corti was ridiculous, he looked at her with interest. There was intense power in her eyes, her mouth was a scandalous gash.

"I have not lied," said the Commissaire. "This is for you."

"Well, not too gay," said Corti, lighting a cigarette and looking at the girl.

"Do your dance, Aisha," said the Commissaire.

"Ah?" said the girl, leaning forward.

"The dance with the snake."

She danced and Corti watched her.

"It will take a good deal of work to get any results."

"But worth it."

"With immense patience, perhaps."

"I would not bring you all this way to show you just a girl," said the Commissaire, with hurt in his voice.

"I am not blind," said Corti. "I am trying to think."

"Look at her eyes."

"Yes, I am looking at her eyes."

"She is intelligent," said the Commissaire.

"Perhaps," said Corti.

"You are the professor, the master, and what is there to lose?"

"Time," said Corti. "Besides, what are the conditions?"

"There are no conditions. She comes, and if it doesn't work out she goes back." He turned to face the girl. "Aisha," he said.

"Ah?"

"You will be taken away from here."

"Ah?"

"Well, the intelligence seems to be confined to her look. Maybe she has a fever."

"No no no," said the Commissaire. "She is scared. She thinks she will be taken to jail, or beaten, or shipped away."

The Commissaire sat on his haunches, and said:

"Aisha, listen, this kind gentleman, my friend, you understand, Monsieur Miomo Corti, owns a very fine cabaret, and you will go there, and dance. Do you understand?"

Yes, she understood. The unbelievable eyes shone like large round coals. The Commissaire looked at Corti.

"If you are searching for sex, here it is."

"I am in search of beauty."

"And Ali?" asked Aisha, holding up her hungry python.

"Ali comes along, of course," said the Commissaire.

She held the snake's head to her large, red mouth and kissed it.

Corti shook with revulsion.

"Well, that is all then," said the Commissaire.

"Does she have the address?"

"We take her along, and the python too. Have you a basket for Ali? Or a trunk?"

The snake had a trunk which was below. And so Aisha, with Ali inside a large black trunk, changed from the misery of the Arab quarter to the glory of the Relaxez-Vous.

On the drive over, Miomo Corti thought of how to present the girl and Ali. He stirred in all the pots of his imagination. Something cold like Siberia in the backdrop. Baudelaire. Here tender evening, friend of the criminal . . . the night comes as my accomplice . . . with the silent step of the wolf . . . and man changes into a wild beast . . . demons, prostitutes, savagery, jealousy, murder . . . insanity.

One could paint with passion and fire here. His mind jumped to crows, to funereal scenery, to hot, to cold, to Nietzsche, to a painting by Franz von Stuck called "Sin," to Hamlet, to jungle, to the black horizon of Death, to everything troubling mankind.

They were driving toward the bridge that leads over the Seine, when Corti said:

"Will she mind, this flame, if I put her up in the basement?"

"She will do whatever you ask of her. She will be grateful. You decide on everything, she is yours."

"And the snake?" Corti asked Aisha.

"Ah?"

"The snake, what about the snake, what about food for the snake?"

"Ali?"

"Oh, he used to get a rabbit, once a week," said the Commissaire.

For a rabbit once a week for Ali, a cot in the basement, her food, and the costumes he would decide on, which would be most probably her black hair and her nougat-colored skin, Aisha became a member of the cast of the Relaxez-Vous.

The rehearsing began with fury. And Gala had some rest.

11.

Just the Family

AISHA HAD LEARNED HER ROLE, it had not even been necessary to slap her into it. The reason was chiefly Ali. The python attached himself to her body like an immense mobile piece of Oriental jewelry, his head weaving over the top of her head and always close to her face, and, as in the case of all reptiles, he seemed ever ready to strike. Besides that Aisha herself was alert, she anticipated, and she had the Arab intelligence and subtlety; she created her act. Miomo Corti merely conducted the séance in his black von Karajan sweater.

As a reward Miomo Corti gave her second billing and moved

her from the basement up to the mansarde, to a small room where on a windowsill and a narrow ledge Ali could sun himself and speculate about birds and cats and fat pigeons.

It was the last day before opening night. Herr Doktor Ueberlinger was massaging Gala. All was ready and Aisha and Ali's number was properly rehearsed and set to a recording of tribal music. Doktor Ueberlinger said:

"Since that snake is in the house, it smells like a jungle."

"Yes," said Madame Michel, "but it's not the snake, it's Aisha. It's the scent of the Arabs."

"Why don't you send her over to the Mother Superior to take a bath?" said Miomo Corti.

"You can't wash that away. A bath will only bring out more of it. Have you ever washed a lion? Or a dog? Well, they smell more like what they are when you give them a bath."

"And when and where did you ever give a lion a bath?" asked Doktor Ueberlinger, who was washing his hands.

"It's not easy," said Madame Michel. "Especially in an ordinary bathtub. I kept her as a pet. I love all animals, but one day my wife said to me, 'I have had enough now. It's either me or that cat, you either get rid of it at once or I leave.' And since I love my wife I got rid of that sweet beastie. She was the sweetest, dearest lioness and only five months old. It almost broke my heart."

"How did you come into possession of a lion?"

"At the time," said Madame Michel as she dusted the room, "I was a man. I was a strong man working at the Circus Medrano, and one of the lionesses there had babies, and I took the smallest of the litter home with me. It makes me sad to think of it."

"Why did your wife object?"

"Oh because she is a realist like all women. And as she grew, the lioness started to eat us out of house and home. She had a terrible appetite. This reminds me — I must go out to buy some food for us. Let us, just the family, for one evening sit together around a table, like civilized people, and eat a decent meal, enjoy the smell of cooking, drink a good glass of wine, and celebrate. God knows we deserve it."

"Deserve it we do," said Miomo Corti, "but when do we have time to do this?"

"Tomorrow, after opening night, when the show is over."

"And whom do you include in the family?"

"Oh well, there will be Gala and you, then me, then the Herr Doktor Ueberlinger, and naturally Monsieur Finsterwald, Aisha, the Mother Superior, King Dagobert, and Professor Clayborn."

"Hold on there. All right, you and me and Gala. The Herr Doktor is against stuffing himself."

"Yes," said the Doktor, "I will join you and thank you for thinking of me, and sit with you, but it is against my principles to eat meat and make a pig of myself."

"That's fine," said Corti, "one pig less."

The Doktor was, however, touched by being included in the family circle and invited, and he was mild and modest with his hands on Gala's body; he was now at the trapezius muscles.

"Now then," said Miomo Corti. "As for Aisha, she eats with her hands, seated on the floor, and she is really not one of us. And then she has seen a good deal of Finsterwald — I suppose it's the python that is the bond between them. They are off limits. They can go to some Arabian restaurant and eat couscous. The Mother Superior has to turn in early. Of fleas and

107

lice we have no need—that lets out King Dagobert. He can celebrate with the Professor under the bridge, with their special pâtés and vintages which we can't afford even the ice for. Now let's see—we will then be three for supper tomorrow night."

"Yes, strictly en famille," said Gala and stretched and yawned.

"I will bring my own food," said the Herr Doktor with persistence and a flash of the yellow horse teeth.

Monsieur Corti picked up the paper to study the announcement. Carmen Tessier mentioned the opening of the Relaxez-Vous in her column on the front page of *France-Soir.*

"Turn over, please," said the nature apostle. Miomo Corti lowered his paper.

"Where is Aisha?" asked the Herr Doktor.

"She went out to buy a rabbit for Ali," said Corti.

The masseur finished his work, covered up Gala, washed his hands, and prepared to take off.

Miomo Corti went down to the cabaret to count the chairs for the hundredth time, and to see if he could jam in some extra seats. The promise of the show had advanced to the point where all the portiers of the hotels offered to pay double for seats. He went to the stage, inspected the lights, the properties, a garden bench, the costumes, he played a record and checked the sound and the lights. He opened the black trunk to see if Ali was in there and closed it quickly, for he was.

It was like the old days; he smiled grimly and recited Baudelaire. Once more he counted every chair. Then he went out into the street and looked up to the towers of Notre Dame. The stars were out and they stood right for him. All man's thinking, all the universe is but a panopticon, a Louvre, a warehouse for the artist who is different from the rest of men, for the images he creates. And he, Miomo Corti, had created that which was sublime. He was in rare harmony with the universe.

That is he was for a brief moment until he saw Aisha coming around the corner and stopping to look into the taxidermist's window. In her honor there was a hooded cobra exhibited and a collection of Arabian musical instruments. The cobra, which was stuffed, came out of a basket. And Monsieur Finsterwald slid out of his shop and with a very unrestrained gesture of the hand invited Aisha into the dimly lit and musky interior. She carried a small basket.

Monsieur Finsterwald pointed to it and asked:

"The rabbit?"

"Yes," said Aisha. "The poor rabbit. I bought him some carrots for his last meal. Look." She opened the lid. A white rabbit of medium size with red eyes was contentedly munching.

"You are very kind. He is happy and you look miserable."

"Oh," said Aisha, "it is a terrible thing. It must be a live one. I buy him, quickly, and I run to take him home, and then I put him in the trunk with Ali and shut the lid and sit on it. And after a while I look and Ali is there, and the rabbit is gone, no sound, no blood, hair, or bones, nothing. It's over. All the same, once a week I suffer."

"For a rabbit it's not a bad ending. And it's decent of you not to watch its agony and to let it all happen in the dark. There are people who enjoy the sight of suffering, who are fascinated by torture and cruelty and death."

The Herr Doktor joined them and talked about nature, and he asked if Aisha had not tried to feed the python some other meals, like milk, or honey, or fruit. He explained that even cats ate bread when they were hungry enough.

"No," said Aisha, "he only eats living creatures."

"Like Miomo Corti," said the taxidermist. He gave Aisha some sweet Arabian candy. She ran back to the house, for once without her snake and with only a rabbit for protection. She ran into Miomo Corti and his loose hand. He served her a loud slap.

"Ah?" she said.

"Just to remind you," he said, but offered no further explanation.

12.

Opening Night

"BON APPÉTIT," said the masseur with disgust. He watched Madame Michel making her last preparations so that all she had to do later was put things in the oven. It was like a gypsy camp, or circus life.

Doktor Ueberlinger was giving Gala a last quick going over.

"You're going to let her eat all that?" asked the nature apostle.

"Well, just a little," said Miomo Corti, who was in a benevolent mood, with money in his pocket.

"I'm going to run out to buy a few more things," said Madame Michel, and left.

111

"She's in perfect shape," said the Doktor giving Gala a last slap. "Now go to sleep. Get a good rest." He covered her up.

Miomo Corti drew the curtains. He went over the list of reservations once more and checked everything. The laundress came with his newly laundered starched shirt, white tie, and stiff collar. He dressed and waited and counted money, and gave Gala a last talking to. Then the hour suddenly was here.

All the windows on the street were filled with people looking out of them. In Paris there is an adventurous and curious public. The place, bathed in light, was filling. Monsieur Corti, in white tie and tails, was receiving the guests at the door.

One Rolls-Royce after another arrived and from the biggest stepped the important clients of that evening. Among the first arrivals was Vittorio Vivanti, the little giant, the human volcano, the Milanese millionaire, with a ravishing Parisienne on his arm, the kind one sees in the Dubonnet ads. As usual without a neck, and with the head of a tadpole, Vivanti looked close to having a stroke. His bulging eyes turned in all directions. He smiled. It smelled right. It looked good. His mouth was wide open, running from ear to ear. He greeted friends. The well-nourished man pushed his way through the crowd and waved, his companion trotted after him. There were all the people that mattered — Rothschilds, Academicians, *le beau monde de Paris*, the international set, everybody. Adorned with medals and insignia, in his best parade uniform, the Commissaire de Brigade Mondaine was near the entrance with the Mother Superior. All languages were spoken. A blue cigarette cloud softened the scene. It could only be a success.

Doktor Ueberlinger and the taxidermist arrived, both in dark suits. There was a strict control over tickets at the door, and they found themselves in the rear, almost in the small kitchen. People stumbled over the chairs to their tables, on every one of which stood two bottles of champagne at 100 new francs each. Waiters in shirt sleeves stalked about, opening bottles and collecting the bills in advance. The Duc de Deauville and his son Armand Comte de Roquefort arrived with their friends. Miomo Corti still held the curtain for a group of most important spectators who had front-row tables. Rich Greeks, more dukes, counts, and important Ritz-type Americans were expected to arrive.

Suddenly an ovation went up from the crowd of pensive nose-pickers, teen-agers, beggars, onlookers, policemen, and neighbors pressing against the entrance. From the largest made-to-measure royal blue Rolls-Royce jumped a footman, who ran around the back and opened the door, and from an interior of beige leather and crystal light fixtures came a figure of dazzling radiance. In ceremonial sheets and turban, with rings upon rings on his fingers, beautifully bearded and mustachioed, stepped a sultan, a pasha — or a maharajah. Whatever he was, he sailed into the Relaxez-Vous like a splendid boat breaking out its spinnaker, big as a cloud. He was conducted to his table. He wore dark glasses under his jeweled turban, his face was of dark, pock-marked skin, and over his immense nose the skin was like that of a dried snake. His attendants had seats in back of him. He used two chairs — one for himself, the other to put his things on. As all Arabs do he carried a kind of handbag of very expensive leather.

At the last moment Professor Clayborn arrived, and with him King Dagobert in his ragged majesty. It began to look like a costume party. The Professor was immaculate in white tie and tails, and there was a lot of arm waving toward him in the audience.

"There is Jeb—"

"Jeb who?"

"Why, Jeb Clayborn. Where have you been, sweetie? How have you been?"

The sultan turned and looked at the curious couple and then inspected the place.

"What an honor," said Miomo Corti to King Dagobert. "I did not expect you, but I will find a place—" He motioned toward the rear of the jam-packed room.

"Thank you," said the Professor. "Thank you very much, but we have tickets, we bought our places." Miomo Corti looked at the tickets and then showed them to a table in the second row center.

The Mother Superior came into the cabaret and the Commissaire asked for silence. The Mother Superior took a canister from the sleeves of her habit and shook it loudly. A few coins rattled inside it. The people turned and looked at her. The Commissaire announced in his most authoritarian tone:

"The good Mother collects for the poor. Give generously. It's for a good cause!"

People twisted in their seats searching for money, and everyone gave. The houselights went down. Miomo Corti appeared on the stage. The audience applauded. He bowed and said: "I will not take your time, dear spectators, telling you how fortunate you are to be here. I open the program herewith.

"Relaxez-Vous welcomes you!

"Amuse yourselves!

"I introduce the first number—inspired by this neighborhood—'Quasimodo.'"

The curtain sailed up. Corti stepped aside and there was a desperate cry from the side of the stage.

"Esmeralda! Esmeralda!" From the left appeared a green, twisted dwarf with lantern and clanking chain, crying, "Esmeralda! Esmeralda!" There was a thunder-and-lightning effect against a backdrop showing Notre Dame.

"Esmeralda! Esmeralda!" he kept crying as he clanked his chains across the stage and disappeared. Then he came back, carrying a lovely girl, limp and with her blond hair hanging down. He carried her like a sack over his shoulder.

She was nude but for the briefest scarf of sea-green, transparent gauze. He carried her to the center of the stage and carefully laid her down in front of where Vivanti sat. She lay with her legs toward the audience. Quasimodo placed the lantern between her legs, took a cigarette from his leather jerkin, and pantomimed a request for a match. He looked in all his pockets for a match and could not find one. Then his face lighted up. He fell to his knees, bent down between the girl's legs, and lit the cigarette from the lantern's flame.

He picked up the girl, and put her over his shoulder and disappeared with his lantern and his chains. The appreciative audience clapped hands at this feat of vulgarity, inventiveness, and superb skill.

"Bravo! Bravo!" they called and looked at each other with smiling faces. It was off to a good start.

The Mother Superior said: "I think I'd better go now."

The "Quasimodo" number was applauded because the performance was given by an immensely skillful contortionist, playing the parts of both Quasimodo and Esmeralda — encased in one costume. The left side was the hunchback, the right the girl.

Inside the double-faced costume was Madame Michel.

The Commissaire was still laughing.

The dressing room backstage was the size of a small delivery truck. In it were costumes, a dressing table and a mirror, also the trunk in which the python was kept. A strong, naked light bulb, hung on a wire, lit up the whole. Madame Michel was getting out of the Esmeralda-Quasimodo costume and putting away her chain and lantern.

Miomo Corti stood by as the next act got ready. He put the jungle music on the turntable and manipulated the lights. If he had shot a cannon into the audience it would not have had more effect.

Aisha did her dance without any costume but the coils of the python. The audience was transported, they asked for two encores. Even Miomo Corti applauded. Vivanti's eyes almost fell from his head. Only the sultan remained aloof. It was too close to his domain to excite him.

Backstage Madame Michel, who now looked like a little withered old man, was transforming herself into an overdressed Parisienne of advanced years, a pleasure seeker. She slipped on sheer stockings, put on a wig, a chic hat with little flowers, high-heeled shoes. Corti was dressing up as a gentleman thief with top hat, gray cutaway, cigarette holder. Gala was making up in the same mirror. Aisha came and put the serpent in his trunk. It all was like a silent wrestling match, urgent, nervous, and desperate.

Madame Michel carried a park bench onstage. The curtain went up, Madame Michel sat there coquettishly with a handbag by her side, sunning herself in the spotlight. Corti, as the thief, approached. He sat down at the end of the bench, seeking her acquaintance. With elegant motions he came near her, and with slow fingers he got hold of the lady's handbag, opened it, and pantomimed to the audience that except for an endless inventory of junk which he unpacked it was empty. He moved closer and put his arm around the lady, who at first resented his advances. She was Hauteur. She showed all the hurt vanities that French ladies can summon upon being accosted, but she was coy in repulsing him. But then she allowed him to kiss her hand and kiss his way up toward her cheek. He played this with white-faced seriousness. His unhappy eyes turned toward the audience. He was a great clown.

While he kissed her, and held her close, his free hand searched in her bustle; then he put his hand into her décolletage at her left bosom, and finding nothing there moved his hand into her right bosom. She neighed like a horse, she made sounds of outrage but she was melting under his caresses. He leaned over her, and continued his search more intimately beneath her mauve velvet skirt. During this scene the street musician played "Die Forelle" by Schubert on his concertina. Madame Michel was an exquisite comedienne and pantomimist and knew her art to the last nuance.

While the street musician wheezed on his leaking concertina, the thief approached his victim even more directly. Like an enraged cow, Madame Michel rose into the air, trying to keep her flower-laden hat on with one hand and her skirts down with the other. She achieved an uproarious effect. She twisted and

neighed with delight when he succeeded in his shameless approach. At the same time she let out squeaky, shrill cries of
anguish. he rummaged among the straps in an old-fashioned,
beribboned corset region of the respectable lady's abdomen.
They both rolled off the bench which stood on end and fell on
the floor. Suddenly the gentleman thief asked: "You are not
hiding anything from me, madame?"

She answered sternly, "Certainly not, monsieur!" and then
added with coquetry and downcast eyes, "But please continue
and I will write you a check." Blackout.

This brought down the house. It was in the classical tradition
of the Parisian cabaret.

The sultan laughed, so did the Commissaire, and everybody
applauded.

Miomo Corti came on stage and raised his arms. The great
moment had come. He announced the next number. He presented Gala, the one and only, the most beautiful creature on
earth, the incomparable who would do a creation of his own, to
the music of Chopin and the words of Baudelaire. The red
curtain rose.

She was silhouetted, she was a statue of marble that came to
life. The audience was absolutely still, it was what they had
come for. Toward the end of the act a joker shouted, "Silence,
please," into the absolute stillness, and this brought a release of
the spell. Tumultuous applause started.

The sultan clapped and said: "I am spellbound!" Corti did
not permit any bows, the curtain remained closed. Signor
Vivanti got up and shook Corti's hand. "That is all I came to see,
you have nothing to worry about. My congratulations and that

Arabian girl is a sensation. She's beautiful and you are a lucky man."

The sultan was still clapping and shouting "encore," the entire audience shouted "encore," and Corti gave the signal and the turntable music started again. Once more Corti recited the poem by Baudelaire and Gala did the number, and with equal effect.

Backstage again before her mirror, Gala applied new make-up to her face and body under the light of the naked bulb which was suspended from the ceiling. In back of her, touching her, and with her properties hanging all about, was Madame Michel. This talented artiste was now again a small withered man, making up in the same mirror as a female impersonator. She gradually transformed herself into a Toulouse-Lautrec figure of Yvette Guilbert in advanced years. She achieved an exact copy of one of the paintings of her, and as little as Gala had by way of costume, namely only her strip of cat fur, as much had she.

She was reaching for her corset, her false bosoms, her feather boa headdress, her high-button shoes, stockings, umbrella, and trying to get her face in the mirror to apply the colors of the painting to her face.

The curtain parted again. The sultan was settled back in his chair. The figure of the Toulouse-Lautrec singer came forward to the applause of all the others. With perfection she rendered the music hall ballads of the Moulin Rouge days, and was asked for two encores. If Gala had not been on the program again as the next attraction, she could have sung all night, for she was a superb Parisian music hall singer.

When Madame Michel came backstage she said to Gala:

"Your fortune is made. The sultan is beside himself, he has eyes only for you, he looks at you like something wonderful to eat. I know him from the Scheherazade. Don't ruin your chances. He'll take you to Beirut or wherever he comes from. He has a palace in Paris, another on the Riviera. He has billions, he showers fortunes on women he likes."

The music started for the next number. Gala went on to deafening applause. It seemed as if the sultan was going to climb on the stage. Gala finished her number and gave two encores and then came the intermission. Nobody left. The show was a success.

13.

Mohammed

DURING THE INTERMISSION the audience of the Relaxez-Vous could exchange opinions, look at the objects on the walls and the ceiling, wait for the surprises to come, and fill their glasses and light their cigarettes.

The sultan turned to one of his aides and that man got up and wound his way out of the audience and then came backstage. He inquired of Miomo Corti if Gala could have supper with the sultan after the show, wording this in the proper language of such proposals.

Madame Michel punched Corti in the ribs and said: "Now don't spoil everything."

"Yes," said Corti, "tell His Highness he can have supper with Gala—here."

"Here?" asked the aide. "We did not know."

"Oh yes, we serve excellent food here," said Madame Michel.

"Yes, here," said Corti to make sure. The aide left.

The sultan was delighted. He sent the aide back to inform Gala of his joy.

After a presentation of "Le Mort Joyeux" and another group of songs by Madame Michel as Yvette Guilbert, the show came to an end. Everybody was elated, everyone left happily. The waiters changed clothes and went home. Only the sultan remained. Madame Michel, still in costume, was in the small kitchen basting a pheasant. Monsieur Corti spoke to the Commissaire who shook him by the hand and patted him on the shoulder.

"Nothing objectionable, I hope. You have been content?" asked Corti.

The Commissaire said: "I congratulate you. Piquant, perhaps, and not for children, but in excellent taste. I have had a lovely evening."

A table was set, with a tablecloth and a silver stand that had fruit on it. The sultan was directed toward it. He sat down.

"For whom is the third place setting?" he asked, pointing to the table.

He was informed that it was for Monsieur Miomo Corti, the owner of the Relaxez-Vous, who was his host.

"I have not invited him," said the sultan simply, and waved the setting away. He stuck a grape in his mouth and said he wanted to eat alone with Gala and only the musician should stay.

Miomo Corti approached the table with deep bows. He said: "Forgive me, Your Highness, but Gala is a married lady; moreover she adores her husband."

The sultan spat some grape pits into his hand, rinsed his fingers in the champagne bucket, and said:

"Of nil importance, she is the woman that interests me."

Miomo was about to have a Corsican attack of temper and rise in the air with his fists up. Madame Michel grabbed at his coattails and, thanks to her strength, pulled him to the back of the room.

"Don't be a fool, Miomo," she said. "Don't spoil everything! That one is really rich. He owns all the sand of the Sahara and the oil, and he has houses and palaces and millions. I know him from the old places. Play it right, for once. Make him pay. He will come every night, he will buy the place. Think of Gala, he will shower her with furs and jewels, and pay anything you ask for."

Corti sighed deeply and ran his hands through his hair.

"Just let me handle it," said Madame Michel, and approached the table smiling.

"When is she coming?" the sultan asked impatiently.

"She will come, Your Highness," said Madame Michel.

"What is there to eat?"

"It takes a little time, Your Highness, for here everything is cooked to order," said Madame Michel, and excusing herself ran into the kitchen.

The sultan clapped his hands. The musician started to play "Je suis le vagabond, le marchand de bonheur."

Monsieur Corti came running from one side — and Gala from the other.

"Ah, here you are!" said the sultan getting up. To forestall any crisis Madame Michel came running back with a candlestick and started to light the candles.

"That is better," said the sultan. "Now I can see her. Here, sit down, my dear, next to me. On my right."

Gala asked her husband if she could sit down. She was demurely dressed in a buttoned-up long dress without any frills or embroidery. The sultan enwrapped her with his gaze. He pulled out the chair.

"Now," he said, stroking his beard, "what do we get to eat? Where is the menu?"

Madame Michel belonged to that class of French people for whom the aristocrat still is the all and everything in this world, and for whom all others have to stand back. The prince, the sultan, the guest, the titled client, the royal customer came first and must be served. She pushed Corti aside once more and said:

"First of all, Your Highness, there is a pâté, a veritable pâté, made by myself, with little squares of truffles."

The sultan listened. He took the hand of Madame Michel, who was still dressed as Yvette Guilbert, and said:

"I have confidence in you, you are charming. What after?"

"A little sole au beurre blanc." Madame Michel closed her eyes and said: "Wait until you taste it. You will forget about all the fish of the sea you have ever tasted. But let me give you the rest of the menu, Your Highness. There is a pheasant, stuffed with chestnuts and cooked in cabbage. That is wonderful for pheasant, there is no better way of cooking it."

"And to drink? What is this champagne? I have never seen it before."

Madame Michel started to excuse the wine but was relieved by Corti, who came forward and said:

"A special reserve of the house, bottled solely for the Relaxez-Vous, as Dom Perignon is for the Pope. You cannot obtain it anywhere else."

"Ah," said the sultan, "there are times, there are nights in life, alas too few of them, which are perfect, which one never forgets, and this promises to be one of them. This place, this wonderful mood, this music, and this wine and supper, all of it is perfect."

The musician pressed down on his keys and started that bath of melodies in which there is the heartbeat of Paris, the sum of one's unhappiness, the promise of love, the sweet fatigue of amorous fulfillment and mystery.

"I have had enough! I have had enough! All is ruined!" said Miomo Corti.

"Go and open the wine at least," said Madame Michel.

She brought in toast and the pâté and a little pot of hot water, for in cutting pâté the knife gets stuck if the pâté comes in a bloc surrounded with aspic. Corti served the wine as Madame Michel cut the pâté.

"A lovely couple," said the sultan to Gala, smiling at Corti and Madame Michel with admiration. Then he gave his attention to the pâté.

In the kitchen, Herr Doktor Ueberlinger was using one of the four small burners of the little oven to heat his pot of soybeans.

"You can have some of these," he said to Corti. "They contain iron, vitamin B complex. Very good for you, good for nerves, very important for the body. All the energy you need."

Corti ignored him. He was now cruising around in the shadows and observing the sultan and Gala while Madame Michel prepared the fritters.

At a table in the back of the bar, from where he could keep an eye on his wife, Corti and the nature apostle finally sat down. Corti ate the leftovers of the pheasant and drank, while in front the musician played with closed eyes and the sultan looked into the eyes of Gala.

"Please call me Mohammed," he said.

"She's going to get a massage tomorrow, like she never had," said Corti, and the Doktor, who was crunching on a Knaekebroed, showed his yellow teeth, swallowed some milk, and said: "You can be sure of that, I promise you."

Gala's appetite was a delight to the sultan, especially when she lost all reserve at the appearance of the fritters with vanilla sauce. She ate until the plates were clean.

"My compliments, madame," said the sultan. "One always eats well in a place where there is harmony. I have never had a better dinner. May we have another bottle of wine?"

"Another bottle of champagne," Madame Michel said to Corti, as she carried out the dishes.

"I can't stand it any more," said Corti.

"I'll get the wine, you go out and get some fresh air to clear your head, or you'll ruin everything."

"That disgusting old Arab," started Corti.

"Now don't behave like a dirty little bourgeois. Leave them alone, and at least let that half-starved girl finish her meal in peace. What is the matter with you?"

Mohammed was smiling. Gala had the rare sensation of food in her stomach and with the wine that had been forced on her, her inhibitions had gone. She said:

"Your Majesty, may I ask you a question?"

"Of course," said Mohammed.

"A very personal question, Your Highness?"

"Oh, ask me anything you want, please."

"Do you have a harem?"

"Oh yes, I have a large harem."

"How is it to have a harem?"

"Oh, it is terrible."

"Can you tell me why?"

Mohammed thought for a while and took a drink.

"How can I best explain it to you? Let me see—have you ever gone for tea to the Hotel Ritz here on the Place Vendôme side?"

"I have never gone to tea anywhere," said Gala.

"If you ever do, then you know what I mean when I say that it is like my harem. It is filled with old crocodiles of women. That is exactly like my harem is, for, unfortunately, you see in a harem women get very old and fat and ugly."

"But could you not get yourself young ones?"

"Oh yes, of course I could, but I do not have the heart to do this, for the old ones would tear the young ones into pieces and scratch their eyes out, out of jealousy. Oh, believe me, it is terrible."

"So what do you do then?"

"I come to Paris and hope to meet someone like you. I would like to see you again. I have a house here. I will give you my address and telephone number and I hope you will come and see me. Tonight has been a happy time." He spoke to her quietly and then he left.

"Now what?" said Corti. "My evening is completely ruined."

The sultan's aide left royal tips and asked for the bill to be sent to an address on the Rue de la Faisanderie.

Gala went upstairs, Corti after her. He grabbed her by the hair and slapped her around for a while, harder than usual.

"But I didn't do anything."

"The way he looked at you all night."

"I don't know how he looked at me, and how could you tell with him wearing those dark glasses?"

"What did you arrange with him, tell me?" He slapped her again.

"I swear to you, nothing." She repeated the conversation.

"He didn't even touch my hand. He is a nice and kind gentleman and lonesome."

"Oh yes, I know," said Corti.

Downstairs Madame Michel looked for Aisha whom she found sitting with Ali.

Under the bridge the Professor was still awake.

"She is usually here at this hour," he said. "I wanted so much to tell her how much I liked the show." The big Rolls-Royce ran up the incline and over the bridge.

"I have wanted to do something for you," said the Professor to King Dagobert.

"You have done a lot for me already, Jeb."

"I want to do something really important. You know it's fine to be a king and free as a clochard, but it gets dull after a while. And you are not young, you're not even old any more. I would like to give you my place up there, my apartment. You can live there in comfort, in warmth."

"And you?"

"I am going away, I am going back to America. My eyes have been opened tonight, I see now where Gala belongs. That is her world. One cannot replace the theater with reality, with a life of home and domesticity and love. I will spare myself the anguish of trying. All things marvelous are unattainable. She belongs to nobody. Maybe she is warmed by the spotlight that shines on her, enfolded by the humid smell of that audience. I know that I would never get her away from this, I could never carry her off. It's been tried so often but it has always failed."

"Think it over before you do anything, think it over well," said the Clochard. "Hold onto the place, you may change your mind tomorrow. You may not leave, or you might want to go back."

The Professor reached into the baby carriage and brought out a bottle of champagne and two glasses and twisted the cork out of the bottle:

"To Gala. Goodbye and farewell."

King Dagobert raised his glass.

"To Gala and to you."

PART THREE

14.

Silent Night

THE STREET WHERE THE HEART LIES was bathed in a gray light. The sky was cloudy, lit by the haze that hangs over the city. The Cathedral was a slate gray.

King Dagobert was sleeping. The Professor sat under the bridge, and the window of the taxidermist's shop was filled with the reflection of a bluish gas light, for Monsieur Finsterwald worked late as always, and like a sorcerer, arranging his objects of nature, brushing furs, polishing and examining crystals and stones, or busy in back welding with his blue flame.

In his active mind there were many chambers; he was part

taxidermist, part jeweler, he welded modern statuary from junk and broken-down motor parts, he gilded, he silvered. In his window he arranged various exhibitions with great care, and they were always worth looking at and held people's attention. The animals brought to him to be stuffed, the ones he found himself, procured from fields, the Bois de Boulogne and the zoos, and preserved for hunters, fishermen, museums and schools, were kept in the window where he exhibited them. In their honor he went to a great deal of trouble to place them in proper surroundings. A large thirty-pound lobster would find himself in a submarine scene with sea shells of great beauty, all of them cleaned and polished to a high gloss. A boar's head was surrounded with autumn foliage and branches. A puma's or a tiger's head found for company a print of the Douanier Rousseau.

Monsieur Finsterwald was as devoted to his subject as Miomo Corti to female beauty, and to this, Finsterwald was also committed. Outlined by the blue light in back of him, Finsterwald stared into the night, down toward the Seine. He opened the door and ran down toward the embankment. He galloped as if afraid of his night shadow. Suddenly he stopped, and in the stammering haste of one who has to speak out in spite of himself, he said to the surprised Clayborn:

"Professor, I must talk to you, I appeal to you, I address myself to your humanity, to the great American heart, to your conscience as a human being. Hear me out. It is all around the neighborhood about Gala and you."

"What about Gala and me?"

"That you are to get married."

"Rest at ease, Monsieur Finsterwald, how could we even if we wanted to? She is married. But what gives you these ideas?"

"Oh, the looks you have for each other, the holding of hands, the nightly visits."

"I am very fond of her and I hope she likes me, but what does it mean to you?"

"She loves you. As for me, it is torture and has always been, it is fire under the ashes. I have thought of hanging myself. I have thought of doing away with myself, but she has no thought of me, in spite of everything I have done. I have run my legs off— whenever there is an auction of furs, of bijous, of theatrical jewelry, I am there, getting new things for her. I create designs, I make the furs over, I have supplied money to keep the Relaxez-Vous going. Not that I am sorry, for I have done it for her, to be near her, to have part in her, to see her, to talk to her, to feel her nearness. She is the only reason for my existence.

"That magnificent fur coat, the white one. It took me twenty weeks of work to get together this coat. It is made of over two hundred white rabbit pelts, and some forty dyed muskrats, to get the effect of a lavish regal mink coat trimmed with chinchilla. It makes her look like an angel floated down from heaven, an almond tree in flower. It blinds you when the light is thrown on it at night. In the daytime, you mustn't look at it, you mustn't look at anything in there in the daytime—"

"Except at Gala."

"Yes, except at Gala. Everything else looks dirty. And is dirty."

"How about her husband?"

"He doesn't count at all, at all. He is not in my way, he is obligated to me. I can close up the place any day and throw him out. I own that house and also this one there—the old one. I have always had the idea, and still have, of someday fixing it up and living in it, if my plans work out—with just a little luck."

"And does she know about it?"

"Lamentably, no. I cannot speak of it, I have never told her or anyone, except you. I have consumed myself with all absence of hope, prisoner of the most terrible solitude, sick with love which eats me like a cancer. Forgive me."

"I am sorry."

"I would ask her but I know the answer. That is I am afraid that she would say, 'Dear Monsieur Finsterwald, I am sorry,' and it would be the sentence, whereupon I would put an end to my days—that or if you married her and took her away."

"I can assure you, there is no danger that I will either marry her or take her away. I couldn't. I adore her. I am very much like you in my feelings toward her, but not so terribly attached," lied the Professor.

"Thank God," said the taxidermist and offered his hand to the Professor. "Do you mind if I talk to you a little?"

"No, no, go ahead if it helps you. I mean, I am very interested. Would you like some brandy? Or some scotch or a glass of wine, or something to eat?" The old baby carriage had become a portable bar, fully equipped with bottles, glasses, ice bucket. It was like something out of the Christmas catalogue of Hammacher Schlemmer.

"Thank you," said the taxidermist. He sat down close to the Professor.

"I must first tell you of what has happened to me." He pointed toward the old house, the one with the bricked-up windows, which he owned. His eyes took on a hypnotic insistence as he talked.

"One never knows what saves one's life. If you are a naturalist, if you have a feeling for animals, if you have observed them all your life, you have some advantages. You can run, jump, and walk like them. We always had dogs, and that is why I am alive today. Excuse me for just one minute." He ran back to his shop, and returned with the skin of a large animal.

"It's the skin of an old dog, a St. Bernard." Finsterwald stroked it with affection and said:

"When it was alive this creature stank so one could not go near it. This old dog was left outside in its doghouse. You know how sentimental the Germans are. I was a privileged prisoner in Dachau, first of all as a taxidermist and therefore useful in preparing things—not animals, people—in the department where they did medical research, and that is how I got into possession of a knife. Also I was more or less free of the routine of the ordinary prisoners.

"The Commandant liked to make jokes with the old stinking dog, when it was alive. When one of the lesser officials had an anniversary or a birthday or promotion, he sent me to bring him the dog as a gift. A large bow was tied to his neck and a bottle of brandy. Of course after a few moments people could not stand it any more and I took him back. That also gave me an advantage in that the sentries used to see me move about. And all the time I planned my escape. One night I crept into the doghouse of the stinking poor old creature, which in this place, where gassing was daily routine, survived on account of these animal lovers. I got sick, not on account of what had to be done, but from the stench of the old animal. I killed it mercifully. Then I worked with feverish haste to skin it, to take this matted, filthy coat off it to wear as a disguise.

"It was freezing cold, but I sweated. A sack hung over the door of its hut to protect it from the cold, but I was afraid to move it. It had all to be done carefully, quickly.

"It took hours, and in the morning—but let me show you. Have you ever seen a better dog in your life?"

He put the skin over himself, and came toward the Professor.

"You can applaud. We are not there any more."

He sat down in his pelt.

"I carefully watched the gates, the goings and comings, and prepared everything. And since my life depended on it I had calculated every move, I had carefully rehearsed the escape. I walked out when it stormed and snowflakes blurred vision, as limping and painfilled as the old dog, in the hour when the prisoners came back from work in the peat bogs. It was almost dark then.

"I came back again to get them used to see me moving about. The guards talked to me in my house, as if I were the dog. Then I went further, and came back later, always careful, always calculating. My greatest fears were the other dogs, the trained German shepherds. I was afraid that one of them would give me away or get loose and fight. They smelled my presence and barked as they passed, but they were held on tight leashes. Everyone was kind to this old dog.

"I had eaten him, all but the bones. I subsisted besides on the food they brought every day and the water. And finally came Christmas Eve.

"That is when I escaped. I had stayed in the dog hut for a

week. It was cramped and most of the time I felt like vomiting—the stench was unbearable.

"I lay with my nose on the ground during the night, near the opening in order to breathe, the dog skin over me. Then it was time to risk it. It was Christmas Eve.

"I could hear them singing 'Silent Night, Holy Night,' in German. In the guardhouse Nazis in festive mood, with jolly faces, took punch glasses in hand and toasted each other. Santa Claus brought gifts and some Gestapo men came, singing, carrying packages, lifting their children up to see the Christmas tree.

"It was Christmas Eve, in Dachau, and the Commandant of the concentration camp and his family and friends were together celebrating. I had calculated every move, and had waited for that night.

"It was bitter cold, and I was as all the others a living skeleton, but I had a disguise and a knife, and as I told you I was a student of nature and a hunter as well as a taxidermist.

"And so I escaped in the shadows, on that holy night of relaxed alertness, of guards singing and bells ringing. I got through, past guards and unsurmountable barriers—that is for anyone not an old dog.

"On that Christmas Eve I loped across the fields being careful of my tracks—and the rest is a long story and not interesting, and neither is the ending. On the way I almost froze to death. I arrived in Paris, no longer a dog, but I kept the pelt out of gratitude.

"From then on, it's another miserable story. The penniless immigrant, old beyond his years, sick, useless, reasoning day and night that it was better to die than to go on without hope, or work, or love.

"I established myself again. I had a new window put into the boarded-up shop—and then one day I saw Gala. She became the light of my life, and by this light I awoke from the dead.

"I don't want to bother or tire you with horrible details, but in Dachau, when they made experiments in survival, and froze people, and tried to get them back to life, the one thing that worked best was to put an almost lifeless man in bed with a girl—that brought him back. Only to look at her warmed me, she lent me strength. This may not mean anything to you. It is all I have to live for. Now you come and take all this away from me.

"Oh, I forgot," said the unhappy taxidermist, smiling sadly. "You are a gentle man, you are not going to. Bless your heart and forgive me." The dog fur slipped from his shoulders, as he took both his hands to shake the Professor's right hand. "The archives of love are filled with curious stories."

He picked up the dog skin. "Good night," he said quietly. And then, as he had come, he ran back to his shop.

"There seems to be a vast society of the adorers of Gala," said the Professor.

King Dagobert sat up.

"It's a cult, she fills the longing of all the little baker and butcher apprentices who bicycle past. She is loved by Madame Michel, by the taxidermist, although I had no idea that he, poor man, suffered so. There is the masseur, there is Signor Vivanti, the clientele of the Relaxez-Vous, not to leave out the Commissaire of the Brigade Mondaine, then Mohammed, then all the passers-by in the street and the ones we don't know about."

"And myself," said the Professor.

"Yes, I know," said the King. "And she loves you."

15.

The Radio Taxi

GALA CAME TO THE BRIDGE.

"Something terrible happened today," she said. "I haven't told Miomo, and please don't you tell him.

"I took a taxi. I always take a cruising taxi, not one who knows me, on the other side of the bridge, to visit Mohammed. I told the driver where to go and the address, and to go quickly and to wait for me, for I knew that if Miomo found out that I visited Mohammed, he'd kill me.

"I gave him the address. At first the taxi driver said nothing. He started his car and looked at me all the time, in the rear-view

mirror, and drove toward the Rue de la Faisanderie. I told him
to make it fast. When we were almost there, he went into a
narrow street, and there he stopped the car.

"I said to him: 'What are you doing here, the house is not in
this street. Why do you stop here?'

"He said: 'She won't go any further. She needs a little rest.
She's out of breath, the engine, it always happens when I am
told to drive somewhere in a hurry. In a little while she will be
all right, but she must get her rest first.' He pushed a small
button, and a small light, not the one overhead, but in a corner
of the old taxi, lit up.

"He said: 'Let me look in your face. You are very beautiful. I
will do you no harm, don't worry.

"'Ah, but you are beautiful!' he said and stroked his cheek,
and looked out, up and down the street. There was no one in
this street. He turned out the light again, then he leaned back
into the compartment. I had on a short skirt. He placed his hand
on my knee and said:

"'I am very lonesome, because a little friend, someone young
and beautiful like you, has gone and left me. I loved her very
much. I like very much to make love, and after I make love, I
feel much better. And you,' he asked me, 'do you like to make
love?'

"I said: 'Yes, I like to make love, but this is not the hour, or the
place.' I took his hand very nicely and put it up, where the taxi is
divided between passenger and driver, and I put my coat over
my knees, folding it, and I said: 'I will give you a good tip, when
we get to the address, but by now your car must be rested and I
beg of you to advance with it.'

"His hand went to my leg again, and he said:

142

"'What do you measure around the bosom and the hips?'

"I was paralyzed with fear and I said: '84 around the chest and 56 around the taille and 90 around the hips and I am one meter and seventy high.'

"He smiled, a hard smile, he had good teeth and his eyes were intense. He said:

"'*C'est une nana bien tournée.*' Nana is low Parisian for a girl," she explained to the Professor.

"I said: 'Are you satisfied now? Can you start this car, please? Now?'

"He got out of the car. He was about thirty-five, big, strong, good-looking, big hands, and bushy eyebrows and a good face. But I was very afraid. He looked up and down the street, he looked very wild. He said: 'I am filled with desire for you.'

"I said: 'Let us go. I am late.'

"Then he started the car. I said: 'I am very content that you are doing this.'

"He said that he wasn't content at all. He said: 'Where are you going? Give me that address again.'

"I gave him the address.

"He said that I was a lady, besides being beautiful, and that he never had seen anyone so *fine* and *jolie* and beautiful, and was I the wife of some rich swine, living off the fat of the land, on the Rue de la Faisanderie?

"I said that none of this concerned him and that I was in a hurry, and he said so was he, and at furious speed he turned down the Avenue Foch past the Rue de la Faisanderie. I pleaded with him. His exhausted car ran along like an express train. He turned into the Bois de Boulogne and then down a path, where he stopped again.

"He said he had to make love, and that he had to do it with me and he didn't care. When this desire overcame him, he could not help himself. He looked tortured, the way the faces of the men are at the Relaxez-Vous when I am on the stage undressed. 'I cannot help myself,' he said, and opened the door. There in the Bois were only the trees, no policemen, nobody. It was dusk and full of fog and shadows and every week one reads that someone is murdered there. He said, 'Come' and offered me his hand.

"I said: "No, I will not come.' He came into the cab and sat down next to me. I said to him: 'Please reflect. You are a chauffeur of a taxi, you are young, you don't have a bad life, you make good money, you are handsome, you will easily find someone to love. Paris is filled with girls, it must not be me.'

"He grabbed me by the shoulders and kissed me. I said: 'Please let me go, I cannot defend myself, you are stronger than I am, and there is no one around. I can't resist, if you take me out of this car. I can do nothing if you will violate me, and kill me.'

"That is how one always reads of it in the paper.

"'The police will find you, you will go to prison and then to the guillotine—and your life is ended, for a few moments of pleasure.'

"He said that those few moments would be worth it, for what else is there in life more wonderful, and anyway he would not kill me, for he loved me.

"I said: 'If you love me then let me go—for what would be pleasure for you would be terrible for me.'

"I was so scared I prayed. He looked at me and I said: 'Please, please, leave me alone.'

"He said: 'I can't bear to see anybody crying,' and I said to him:

"'Maybe you have never said a prayer in your life. Maybe you do not even believe in God. But tonight when you are in your bed you can say to yourself: 'She gave me good advice. Now I can sleep in peace, and tomorrow I can drive my taxi again honestly.'

"He said: 'Yes, yes, I know all that is true. But all the same it is very sad.'

"The wild look had gone out of his eyes and he got out of the taxi and closed the door.

"I said: 'Well, now your car has had her rest again so let's hurry and go. Go on, start. Allons.'

"He said: 'Yes, yes—but allow me, mademoiselle, one last look.' He was back at the wheel; he quickly turned and with both hands took my coat apart.

"I said: 'I have enough of it now, assez! Now go on, or I will lose my temper. I have been patient with you, I have not screamed, or run out of your taxi, or called the police. Go on now! Allons! Move!'

"So he looked mad, pulled his cap down over his eyes, and turned around and drove furiously.

"When we arrived he said he would not wait for me. For he did not want to expose himself to this terrible temptation twice the same day, and that maybe I was right and he would end up a criminal, for one was also locked up for rape. Then he drove off and that is all."

The Professor said: "But how clever of you to tell him the story about prison and the guillotine."

"It's on account of the massages of Doktor Ueberlinger. When Miomo reads all the terrible stories of murder and rape to him, I have to listen to them also. And there was a murder only yesterday in the Bois de Boulogne and they are still searching for the murderer."

"You are very fortunate," said the Professor, "and so are we. One never knows what will happen."

"And what did Mohammed say?" asked King Dagobert.

"Oh Mohammed—he was shocked.

"I said: 'Forgive me, I have just come to let you know that I intended to come,' and I told him the story and he was very upset. He said: 'My chauffeur will drive you back and from now on he will call for you.' I said: 'No, we could not do that on account of Miomo. Please call a radio taxi.' So he said:

"'Oh, I have an idea. I will buy you a car. And then you can come and visit me any time.'

"He is so kind, so gentle—to ask for nothing, and to give. I started to say that it was impossible for me to have a car, I didn't know how to drive—

"'Oh,' he said. 'It will be wonderful. I will have you given lessons. We will drive in the country.' Now I am scared to death.

"He said: 'You can't refuse. It gives me pleasure to do things for you—' and he kissed me on the cheek and he had his butler call a taxi to take me back. And that is the end of it."

The Professor said that he had been shopping at Fauchon in back of the Madeleine, and he had found some very good things to eat.

"Excuse me," he said, "I'll run up and get them. You must be hungry."

The Professor ran up to his apartment. King Dagobert looked at Gala.

"What are you thinking about?"

"I am thinking of that taxi driver. You know, I gave him his tip, and before he drove off, he said: 'Merci, merci beaucoup, mademoiselle. And if you ever need a cab again, call me. My number is twenty-seven.' I will never forget that taxi driver."

"Will you call him?" asked King Dagobert.

"No, of course not, never, but when a man is willing to risk his life for you, that is something."

"Yes—to be loved."

"I would not say this to anybody," Gala said to King Dagobert, "and it is a terrible thing to say, but I can't help myself. Now I almost wish it had happened, that he had taken me and put his arms around me, and thrown me to the ground and made love to me, and if he wanted to, had killed me."

"Here comes the Professor," said King Dagobert.

The Professor came running. He untied a package and took a corkscrew out of the baby carriage; he arranged knife and fork and a plate. She followed his motions with the look of love she had only for him. Then she ate.

"Oh, c'est bon," she said with the grateful dog look. "But I am so scared."

"What of?"

"A gypsy came to the cabaret yesterday. She was looking for work, she asked Miomo if she could pass among the guests and read fortunes. Of course he refused. She said she would read my hand, for nothing.

"I gave her my hand, and she looked at it and then she folded

147

it, closed it, and looked at me and said: 'I am sorry, I cannot tell you what I see.'

"I said: 'I have money, I will pay you.'

"She said: 'No, no.'

"Then she left. I ran after her in the street. She said: 'I am sorry, it's too terrible.'

"I said: 'Nothing can be more terrible than my life. Please, please tell me,' and I forced money on her.

"She said: 'There is a tall, dark man who loves you very much and you will have an accident.'"

"Nonsense," said the Professor. "She wanted to punish Corti by scaring you, and as for the tall and dark part—all people gypsies see are tall and dark, never small and fat. I am tall and dark, and so is Miomo, and so is the taxidermist, the sultan—so is De Gaulle."

"Just the same it's awful," said Gala. "I asked her what kind of an accident I would have and she said: 'An accident with an automobile.'"

"Well, that's very simple. Don't accept the car," said King Dagobert.

The Professor said: "An automobile accident one can have without owning a car. Just walk in the street. You can't stay in bed all day."

"Yes, and I always wanted a car," said Gala.

"Then by all means get it," said the Professor.

"But how will I tell Miomo? My God." She jumped up. "I have to get back." She ran.

"I have a confession to make," said the Professor. "You know why I came down here to live under the bridge?"

"Go on," said King Dagobert.

"Only on account of her. I saw her every evening, I couldn't sleep any more. I tried skiing, I did everything to keep away from her."

"I know," said King Dagobert, and filled himself a glass, and one for the Professor.

16.

The Gift

DOKTOR UEBERLINGER was hanging up his sack and with Madame Michel he started putting the bed on its four wooden blocks, to raise it for his work.

"We should now be able to afford a massage table, a proper folding table instead of going through this every time I come here."

"We will get one," said Miomo Corti. "And we will also have a daily massage on that new table. Look at her! You saw how she ate on opening night. Now the sultan comes here every night and eats and drinks with Gala. I must protect myself. In six months she will be finished. She will look like a Michelin tire ad made of welts and bulges, with no expression on her face, her front, or her rear. All of my labors will be undone. Listen to me, Gala! It will all sink away in fat! in lard! in voluptuousness! These lovely bosoms, that are your most precious possessions and the finest, most perfect, most beautiful in the whole world, and of any race, shade, or color of woman, they will become like cows' udders, your abdomen will sag, you will be a shapeless bag of fat, and no one will care if you take off your clothes or not. At least not the clientele of this place.

"For why do they come? Why are you famous? Why does the sultan come every night? Why does Vivanti make you disgusting propositions? Why does the Commissaire de Brigade Mondaine, who has free access to every cabaret in town, stay here until the end of every performance? Why does Professor Clayborn hang around? It's all because you are the world's most beautiful woman, the most perfect and precisely constructed female. Because completely nude on stage you project the goddess — inaccessible — eternal. You are alone, and each one in the audience is alone and enthralled and captivated, and that is why there is no leering, no snickering, no laughing. You are the dream come true, and they are all glued to you, men as well as women, by the laws of art, love, and passion, by the innermost secrets of nature."

Corti looked at her and said to the masseur:

"She hasn't the remotest idea of what I am talking about. She doesn't think, she looks at me like a calf."

"A poor little calf about to be slaughtered," said Madame Michel. "You can't have her massaged every day. It will kill her."

"Well, she can't eat then — one or the other," snapped Corti.

"Yes, she must stop eating," said the Doktor, "or else I will come every day." He rubbed his hands and showed his foul teeth. He looked like a Nihilist about to set off an assassination.

"I beg of you," said Miomo. "It hurts me more than it does you to see you mangled here and punished, but think for a moment. You are a goddess, a mirage, unreachable, an apparition — something like in a fairy tale. Now what kind of an apparition are you carrying in front of you — a belly? Answer me that. Am I right, Herr Doktor Ueberlinger?"

"Absolutely," said the Doktor and addressing himself to the Idol, he said: "He's right. You are Aphrodite, my dear, risen from the sea, come down from heaven, you are that which man has made for man's desire. There is only one Cleopatra, there was only one Venus, there is only one Garbo, there is only one Gala, and we must preserve her. Now lie down, please!"

The doorbell rang, and Madame Michel went down and signed for a small package, a box from Mohammed.

Gala was stretched out on the bed and covered with the sheet, but she was allowed to open the box. It contained a string of emeralds with a ruby clasp and a note.

"*Wunderbar, dieser Schmuck,*" said the Doktor. Madame Michel put it around Gala's neck.

"Yes, yes, I know," said Miomo Corti. "Very nice, very generous, but that sultan or maharajah or whatever he is, is ruining everything. This will end badly. I know it."

"Now you have everything," said the Doktor, as he put baby powder on Gala's body. "Fame, money, real jewels."

"I have nothing," cried Gala.

"You can have anything you desire," said Corti, with a nervous twitch of his mustache. "Except a five-course dinner every evening. What is it you want? Tell me, just tell me."

"I want a bathroom installed here."

"You shall have it."

"I want some clothes."

"Go and buy all the clothes you want."

"But I need some money to buy clothes."

"One doesn't go in a shop and buy clothes—like meat or vegetables. A person of consequence goes to a couturier, to St. Laurent or Balenciaga, and has things made, and then they send the bill."

"That is fine," said Madame Michel. "But the poor child must have money to take a taxi to go there, and also she must wear something decent. She cannot go in a cache-sexe or your famous marmalade cat G string. Come on now. Give her some money, you miserable mean maquereau."

This unusual and direct request and demand upon him for financial relief brought forth a most unexpected reaction.

Miomo Corti could not stand accusations. He went to the theatrical trunk and got out a box. He handed out money.

"Here, Doktor, for a new massaging table. Here, Michel, for household expenses and back salary. Here, Gala, Goddess of Beauty, Queen of the Night, for your personal use." He stuffed money into her hand. "Is there anything else?"

They were all perplexed and thanked him and excused themselves, for the giving of money is one of the secrets of nature. Madame Michel said that she was sorry about what she had called him; the nature apostle tied his bundle of bills with a rubber band, and put it away in his trouser pocket and smiled, and then massaged Gala to exhaustion. She had more real jewels now than false ones. She bit into the pillow, her small radio played the "Fire Dance" by de Falla, and when he was through with his beating and chopping—when it was all over— Madame Michel said:

"Come, Gala, we'll go shopping."

"I love nothing more than shopping," said Madame Michel, helping Gala into her dress. "When I was done with the underground, and the government of France was ready to award me the highest decoration for heroic service to my country, I said: 'No, no, thank you. I want something much more important.'

"They said: 'Anything.'

"And I said: 'Allow me to change myself into a woman, issue me papers to legalize this so I can go about dressed as a woman.' And that, my child, is the reason I love *La Belle France*—this spirit, this elegance, this understanding and civilized tolerance. Nobody made jokes about it. A commissaire was instructed, and it was so written down in my dossiers, and I always carry the card, which every policeman and commissariat respects.

"So let's go up on the bridge du Pont Neuf, at the statue of Henry IV, where we can get a bus. No use throwing away money. I know some small boutiques, and we will put some things in work. They have little needle-and-thread women there that are alert, and there are most wonderful fabrics, blazing silks, air-weight wool costumes. You'll look like an angel—oh what a pleasure! And then shoes, by an Italian of course." They walked past the Hotel Dieu, the flower market, and the Conciergerie and got on the bus and had a lovely time ordering things in very special places, in every one of which Madame Michel was received with proper respect and given special attention and prices.

They were on a bus on the way back, having made the necessary immediate purchases. Gala was dressed in a gray wool costume, with a white smoke-ring collar and long, white gloves. Madame Michel said:

"Do you remember a few years back? The Christmas windows were filled with glitter the first Christmas after the war — junky kinds of gifts, animals stuffed but not with love, badly done and of cheap materials. The Santa Clauses were also tacky. All was wanting, but it was gay just the same. The wind was blowing outside and to the trunks of the plantain trees they had tied Christmas tree branches, so that everything looked festive. At the corner — but you don't remember any of this — there was an Arab selling chestnuts from a complicated machine. Smoke rose from the wide metal cover that was over the pan, and you stood there with Miomo — you were only a child — and you looked at that pan, and he had no money to buy you chestnuts. Several people waited and the Arab got busy. He was a careful man, he could not sell the chestnuts without his measuring cup and this had fallen into the crate where he kept his cut-up newspapers and the uncooked chestnuts and a knife to split the *marrons* open. You watched all this the way children do. And I watched you, for I had fallen in love with you. Then he found his measuring cup, a tin cup like a beggar's, and he lifted the large lid off the pan and rattled it. A blue-white cloud of vapor rose, and a wonderful scent floated past us. Then he began to take one after another of the chestnuts that were done, and after measuring put them into the newspaper cones, and with a very kind smile he handed them to the customers. I bought some and handed them to you. I was a man then, that is, dressed as one. You ate the chestnuts with more pleasure than anything since. A true thing is a true thing and therefore important and our lives are to a great degree miserable because there is so much falseness around us."

Gala embraced Michel.

"Since then I cared for you and fed you and watched over you as if you were my own," said Madame Michel. "And now tell me what is troubling you."

"Oh, it's terrible, Madame Michel. I don't know what to do."

Madame Michel put her arms around her and she said:

"You may call me just Michel, chérie, and tell me everything and I will give you good advice. Now what is your problem?"

"Mohammed."

"Oh. I know—he wants you to quit Miomo and live with him, to travel with him, to be nice to him, to him alone. You know that can become awfully dull."

"Oh no, none of those things. At least he has not said so. He's a lonesome man, he has never permitted himself any liberties—he just wants to give me things."

"But that is no problem. Let him."

"He wants to give me a car, and I have always wanted a car."

"Fine, Gala, take it. I wish someone would give me a car."

"But Miomo—I cannot hide a car from Miomo—he would never let me drive it. You know he always says that I live like a cat, I sleep and eat like a cat, and I don't think. Do you think, Michel?"

"Of course I think. I think about you, I think about the house, I think about France, I think about De Gaulle, I think about my son and about my wife—and here is where we get off."

The bus stopped in the center of the Pont Neuf in front of the statue of Henry IV. They walked toward the Relaxez-Vous.

"What shall I do about the car, Michel?"

"Tell him, just face him and tell him. Say, 'The sultan wants me to have a car.'"

Next morning Miomo asked with surprise, "A car?" and smacked her. "He wants to give you a car, and you visited him at his house? Why do you always lie?"

"I didn't lie."

"To say nothing and do something behind my back is like lying, no?" He smacked her again.

He started shaving, and he held up the tip of his nose and carefully operated on the thin line of his mustache.

"What kind of a car?"

"Oh, any kind of a car I want."

"And who is going to drive that car?"

"Well, I would."

"You! I will never permit that."

"I can take driving lessons."

"You would never pass, you are much too stupid. It took me years to teach you to carry your bare ass across a small stage. You'll get yourself killed or cut up. You have read about these accidents in the paper."

"I will be careful."

Then he stopped shaving and said:

"We could accept the car. I know how to drive very well."

"Yes, and you could teach me."

"Still, you would have to pass the test to get a license and you never will. You have a brain like a chicken."

"I know people who drive who aren't so very smart—like taxi drivers, for example."

"Well, we'll think about it. Get ready, here comes Doktor Ueberlinger."

The health apostle floated into the room carrying the new folding massage table. He set it up and made preparations while he was informed about the car which Mohammed wanted to give to Gala.

He was of the same opinion as Miomo—to accept the car but not to let Gala drive it. It was too risky to have his priceless, precious porcelain puppet broken.

During the massage séance of that day Miomo Corti ignored crimes of passion and other police reportage and read off one after the other all the automobile accidents in Paris and in other parts of France, and those great car disasters that had taken place in the rest of the world of sufficient horror to be reported in *France-Soir.*

"Maybe it's better to forget about the car," said Gala.

"When is he going to give you that car?"

"Oh, any time I want it."

"What kind of a car?"

"I don't know."

"With his money it should be a Ferrari, or a Delahaye, or a Jaguar, or a Mercedes," said Miomo Corti. "That is the car for me, the Mercedes 300 S.L. with fuel injection and a speed of two hundred and fifty miles."

"Kilometers you mean," said the nature apostle.

"No, I mean miles. It does that on a race track," said Monsieur Corti, who was a lover of cars and a racing devotee and suddenly saw himself at the wheel of this marvelous car.

"You will kill yourself with a car like that," said the Doktor.

"I just want a little car," said Gala, "to drive around in," and then stifled a cry of agony in her pillow. The Doktor had knuckled the small of her back and was moving up toward the trapezius muscles with alternating pressure on the spinal cord and *tapotement* and corkscrew twists.

"You don't want a small car," said Miomo Corti. "An accident in one of those small cars and it's all over, they fold up like handkerchiefs. You are dead, or, worse, in a hospital disfigured for life. And then where are we?"

The massage became furious and Doktor Ueberlinger chopped away on Gala's backside.

"Monsieur Corti is absolutely right. Turn around, please." Corti lowered his paper, and supervised the turning of Gala. The Doktor let the sheet slowly down over her, and took her left leg in work, pressing on the tarsal bones.

"Oh, quiet," said Miomo. "Now, to those people in a heavy car nothing happens. It's like a locomotive, you understand. It's the people in the other car that are hurt."

The masseur was getting his bottle of alcohol for the rub.

Miomo Corti thought for a while. Then he said to Gala:

"Here is your chance at last to do something for me."

"What?"

"Give me a present, something I want."

"I have always given you presents."

Corti folded his arms and said:

"Yes, I know. The embarrassing gifts one receives on birthdays and at Christmas, and of course bought with my own money—for instance, a pipe, and I never smoke a pipe, slippers which I never wear, for I am an active person and not the easy-chair slipper or *robe de chambre* type. Dressing gowns are wasted on me. I think you gave me three. There is really nothing you can give me that I want except a car."

"That is a superb idea, just *wunderbar*," said the Herr Doktor applying alcohol to Gala's bottom and enjoying the round firmness of the two cool half globes, which were his favorite terrain for the lingering, caressing application of his able hands. "He already has everything else he needs, like a wrist watch and cuff links, I suppose, and studs for his stiff bosom shirts and a traveling *nécessaire* — "

"Of black crocodile," said Gala. "That was the gift of our first anniversary, and now I give him only neckties."

"And you have never seen me wear them, for they are in the most atrocious taste. I always give them away."

"So you see how fortunate you are," said the Doktor.

"Thank you, Gala," said Miomo.

It was the first time he expressed a sentiment of gratitude. The masseur slapped her thigh.

To ward off further punishment Gala agreed.

"The car will be in your name," said Corti when the torture was over and the Doktor had packed his stuff and gone on his winged way up to his home. "All right, I give my permission. You can have the car. And I know exactly what kind of a car I want — an American car, a Thunderbird.

"These others are fine for sport alone, but you have to send your baggage ahead, for there is no room for it. You can't even take a dog. They are for egoists or for a honeymooning couple.

"This is a serious car, elegant, impressive. And if something happens, you get it repaired anywhere in the world. If you have ever had an accident in France, a dent in your fender, you know what that means — endless waiting, and expense. With an American car, you drive to the garage and they take off a fender and put another one on — one two three — like that.

"You tell him that you want a Thunderbird. I'll write it down for you."

"What color?"

"The exterior gun metal, the interior red. All my cars were of that color."

"Very smart."

The neighborhood was informed and everyone had a different opinion about the car, and advice to give. The Commissaire de Brigade Mondaine also spoke and said that when the time came for Gala to take the test, then he himself would see to it, through the proper channels, that she passed. He had friends in high places.

"That will be a day," said Corti, "for everybody who values his life to stay home."

"Now it is done," said Gala, on the next nightly visit to the bridge. "Miomo knows about the car and he gave me permission to get it."

The King took plates and a dish from his precious old baby carriage and the Professor opened the wine.

"Here is a sandwich, very American, rye bread and turkey with coleslaw. The American tourist found an American Jewish delicatessen shop where you get rye bread, pickles, and this coleslaw which is cabbage." Gala ate it with delight. She said:

"Mohammed and I went to some automobile salons to look at cars. He said, 'You will pick out one you like,' the way one says to a child in a pastry shop, 'What do you want, a vanilla, chocolate, or strawberry éclair?'

"First we saw some dear little cars, very beautiful too, but the sultan said, 'Oh no, you don't want any of those,' so he told the chauffeur to drive on, and we came to a place where they had immense cars, and he pointed at the biggest, a convertible racer, and said, 'We want that. We also want an instructor with it to give mademoiselle lessons.' As simple as that. But then I said, could we look at a Thunderbird. And we did, and so suddenly I had my car. It is coming tomorrow morning."

Miomo Corti bought himself an English cap and driving gloves at Gelot's, hat makers to royalty on the Place Vendôme, and with the chauffeur sitting beside him, and Gala in the back of the car, gave it a trial run and pronounced it superb.

Then followed three weeks of driving lessons and study and after that the test. Gala came under the bridge and told the Professor and the King about the test.

"Tomorrow the test comes, and our Commissaire has informed the traffic bureau that I am a friend of his. The sultan will also be there to see if he can be of help. I will have my hair done beautifully and put on make-up, and I will wear my new fur coat and put a little perfume under my ears, and I will be very sweet to the man who gives me the test so that I will not fail to pass it."

"It is better to save yourself all that trouble and just give him a hundred-new-franc note. They are all mediocre functionaries and not impressed by beauty," said the King.

"I am very nervous. I hope I will not have an accident."

"Please accept my contribution," said the Professor and handed Gala a hundred-new-franc note. "It will all be simple and you will pass. Don't think about it."

The Professor opened a bottle of wine. The King said:

"Look at all these delicious little things he has got for you, slices of salmon, jambon de Paris, and all the sausages of France, Hungary, and Italy, a taste of each, and here is a galantine of chicken, and a slice of smoked goose, and then a cheese, a little goat cheese, which you like so much. He is running around with his market basket like a housewife to find things for you."

Monsieur Finsterwald came down from his shop, where he now had an exhibit of reptiles—chameleons, an iguana, a moccasin snake—and a ferret, all inspired by Aisha, with whom the taxidermist, who saw the hopelessness of further pursuit of Gala, had started a liaison.

The Professor filled a glass and offered it to Finsterwald, and also offered him the dish of sausages. The taxidermist helped himself.

"When I think of how they are hunting her," he said, holding a half-devoured slice of ham, "all of them, I wonder who will win in the end."

"What do you mean?" asked Madame Michel.

"Vivanti promises her the big time, the world of the cinema, a brilliant career, and life as a star. Not bad, that.

"The sultan opens his heart and pocket to her, and offers a life of travel, horses, cars, palaces, and fabulous riches. Not to be sneezed at either.

"Miomo Corti still holds her by the sacred bonds of marriage, by her naïveté, by her place as queen in the stable of the Relaxez-Vous, and by her faithfulness and whatever mystic power lies in his eyes. Awful, but she seems to thrive on it."

He took a sip of wine and held up his glass:

"And here is the dear good Professor, the knight in shining armor, the kind and decent American, who fights all this with the knives of *charcutiers*, the pickles and sauces and salads of the delicatessens. He approaches it by way of the stomach."

"And you?" asked the King of the taxidermist.

"I am out of the running. I have nothing to offer. I give up. I have no chance. I only await with breathlessness the surprise of the solution, bewildered like one reading a detective story of which the last pages with the solution have been ripped out."

"You forget me," said the King. "This marvelous creature, this skin like velour, this heart, these eyes—do you insult me by saying that I am too old, too gaga, that I am immune to all that?"

"You are the one," said Gala and kissed him.

They ate in silence and the Professor looked at Gala with the sad eyes one sees in railroad stations and piers, and at prison gates—the terrible last look toward the one whom one will never see again.

"Cheer up," said King Dagobert. "All will come out all right."

"I will be very careful tomorrow," said Gala. "I promise you. I like to drive, it gives one a new power, like wings. I am like another person since I have this car. It has given me freedom."

An inspector of the division of motor vehicles of the city of Paris called Gala's name. He had the papers, which were filled out. The car was at the door and there was a relatively open space around the Panthéon in which she executed various maneuvers of left turn, right turn, stop, reverse—and then she drove up a one-way street the wrong way, went through a red light, and parked the car in a forbidden zone.

The sultan sat in his car in front of the Panthéon. He covered his eyes.

"For a beginner, she did better than expected," said the kind inspector, who was not immune to perfume, youth, beauty, and money. They went back into the office, the paper was stamped and signed, and Gala paid the fee. All was in order.

Gala, holding her papers and now licensed to drive, was leaving the door of the bureau when she met the Commissaire de Brigade Mondaine. She bowed and smiled and thanked him, and he said he wanted to see for himself if she was a good driver and able to handle the marvelous machine.

"Allow me," he said and took the wheel. He would drive her out of the worst traffic.

He said: "You don't mind, but around here, one cannot properly judge a new driver. You are new, I mean so young and so beautiful—and beautiful women are seldom serious—and driving is a serious business, especially in a powerful car like this. You can get into trouble easily." So he drove very well and very carefully out along the Seine to the Right Bank, out the Rue Charenton, and out of Paris on the highway. He praised the car. He didn't let her drive at all. The sultan's car followed them.

The Commissaire said: "I will give you some hints. The Parisians drive unlike anyone else in the world. The good driver makes definite decisions and he carries them out with precision. You see that street there? We will turn right. Now you can tell a good driver by the red light of his brake. A good driver does not use the brake, he knows the speed of his car, the road, and he calculates when he comes to the turn. And of course this car has magnificent reflexes. Now watch. You see the bridge? There to the right? We will turn—"

"He turned," Gala said to the Professor that night, "and suddenly I thought the end of the world had come. A big truck at the right of us was in collision with us. It went down the grade, and my beautiful car was smashed—the whole right side of it. Luckily it was like a locomotive—but now it was like a broken locomotive. The Commissaire is in the hospital with a broken leg, and I thank God nothing happened to me."

"Yes, thank God," said the Professor, "but tell us about the car. How did you get back?"

"I forgot to tell you that the sultan was there. He was there at the beginning when the test was going on, with his chauffeur. He also gave the examining inspector an envelope, and when we drove out, he was along, he followed, and when the accident happened, he was there. He wasn't in his white sheets, he looked like someone else, a very small man. One could only recognize him in his dark business suit by the large nose and the dark glasses, and of course by his voice."

"And his kindness."

"Yes, his great kindness. He said not to worry about the car, it would all be very simple and he would take care of everything. And his chauffeur called the police and asked for an ambulance."

"And Miomo, what did he say?"

"Oh, he was very surprised."

"Is that all?"

"That I passed the test."

"Well, he'll be surprised when he reads it in the papers tomorrow."

"It will not be in the papers."

"Thank God that you are safe," said the Professor.

"The gypsy was almost right." Gala embraced the Professor.

"It was a miracle." They were holding onto each other.

"What are we going to do?" asked Gala.

"Hope for another miracle," said the Professor.

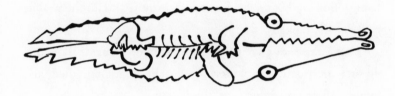

17.

The Virgin

"Look what money can do," said the taxidermist to Lily. The little girl was bouncing her ball against the Relaxez-Vous. "The Commissaire de Brigade Mondaine has been moved to the American hospital and is in the care of the best surgeons. The beautiful car is repaired almost overnight and is as good as new—all for Gala and because the sultan is a rich, rich man."

"It is not enough to be rich. One must also be generous," said Madame Michel.

Madame Michel was washing the already clean car, she was

dusting the hood of the magnificent Thunderbird, and humming while she did it. The neighbors stood around admiring it.

Monsieur Finsterwald, equally attracted, took a chamois skin from a pail, wrung it out, and went over the windshield.

A policeman restrained little boys from climbing on the long sloping rear deck.

Miomo Corti stood watching the adoration from his room, pressed against the window. The emotional manifestations in this man took the form of twitches, of shaking, of nervous contractions of his mustache, his eyebrows, and all the mobile parts of his being.

"I have had enough of playing nursemaid," he said. "It simply doesn't amuse me any more." His shoulders twitched and jumped, first the right, then the left.

Doktor Ueberlinger, with his huge hands folded like a large round Italian bread, sat idly on the bed. Gala was gone. There was nobody to massage. Since Corti had not read the paper out loud that morning, Doktor Ueberlinger bent forward and picked up the copy of *France-Soir* which lay on the floor.

Suddenly his lips parted. He showed his old teeth and looked like one of the masks that represent the figure of Tragedy in theatrical décor.

"Does this say anything to you?" Doktor Ueberlinger pointed with his oversize index finger and a blunt gray fingernail to a boxed announcement in bold type and read:

"VIRTUALLY FROZEN STIFF, A YOUNG WOMAN WAS FOUND UNDER THE PONT NEUF. HER FACE BORE SIGNS OF SLAPPING, HER TEMPERATURE WAS BELOW THAT WHICH NORMALLY SUSTAINS LIFE. SHE WAS DRESSED IN A MINK

COAT AND VIOLET-COLORED SKIING PAJAMAS. TAKEN TO
THE HOTEL DIEU SHE IS RECOVERING, DUE TO HER
YOUTH, AND THE PROTECTIVE GARMENTS. SHE WORE A
WEDDING RING, BUT NO OTHER MEANS OF IDENTIFICA-
TION. IT SEEMS TO BE A CASE OF ATTEMPTED SUICIDE."

The Doktor was on his feet.

"It sounds like Gala," he said. "I will run over to the hospital immediately."

"You are crazy," said Corti, twitching all over. "Look out of the window."

The Doktor looked out of the window.

"What is there to see?" he asked.

"It is spring, and no one freezes to death, you fool," cried Corti. "Look at the date on that paper. Besides, her mink coat is hanging there, and I would never have allowed her to wear violet-colored ski pajamas. Look at the paper. It's old. Madame Michel, who saves every bit of string and old paper, kept it, and when Gala packed her belongings she used some of it."

"You are right," said the masseur. "I never read the papers."

"Why did she leave me?"

"I could give you many reasons."

"Women are strange, anyway. I must face the fact. Now it is like a bad dream, but maybe it is for the best. Besides she was getting out of hand, and not any younger as far as this business is concerned. I will find another one. Paris is full of girls of youth and beauty."

"You'll never find another like her," said the Doktor.

"Leave me," screamed Corti.

"If you should need me, you know where I am."

With his hand on the doorknob, the Doktor said: "I hope she

comes back, she was like a Hindu idol. I worshiped her. My life will be empty without her."

The masseur had tears in his eyes. Miomo Corti, who had no tear ducts, but did have poetic appreciation, asked in a hollow voice:

"What did you say she was like?"

"Like a Hindu idol," said the masseur.

"Women," said Corti, "are like money, very desirable, and they can do things for you only when you don't have them. When you have them they are like money of no value and only a bother."

The Doktor said goodbye softly and closed the door. Corti sank on his chair and looked out of the window.

Below, the Doktor stopped at the taxidermist's shop. Monsieur Finsterwald, with a stuffed crocodile in his hand, was talking to Madame Bernard:

"The love life of animals is curious and interesting and sometimes infinitely more tender than that of man. You take the crocodiles. When they make love, the male turns the female on her back, just as man does. But, at the end, when he is done he turns her back again."

Madame Bernard asked: "Why?"

"Because," said the taxidermist, "she cannot turn herself and would die."

"How nice of him," said the laundress.

"It is," said Doktor Ueberlinger, "merely in the scheme of nature and has nothing to do with love," and then he began to tell them of the condition of the ménage at the Relaxez-Vous.

The Mother Superior passed and heard the terrible news.

Then came little Lily and the Professor. They formed a group of sad faces outside the shop of Monsieur Finsterwald.

Below, under the bridge, King Dagobert, with the minuscule end of a cigarette stuck to his lower lip, was rolling up his mattress.

Miomo Corti called for Madame Michel.

"Go," he cried. "Run and fetch King Dagobert, the only good friend I have, the only man I can trust."

The siren of a Seine barge howled as it came around the bend. Madame Michel was running toward the bridge.

She said: "He wants to see you, he wants to talk to you. I don't know what is the matter with him, he looks awful. He's been up most of the night. That is, both you and I know what is the matter, but he thinks that he—" she looked up toward the Professor's place "—wants to steal her from him, or has already done so. Well, she wants to be stolen, and one cannot blame her, poor girl. She is gone, and nobody knows where. I fear that if you drag the Seine, that is where you will find her. He is in the deepest pit of black despair and asks you to come to talk to him. He thinks maybe you know something. He says that you are the one good friend he has."

"What gives him that idea?" said King Dagobert as he got up and followed.

Miomo Corti was sitting on the chair swathed in his elaborate dressing gown, his head in his hands.

"Well the birds are still here," said King Dagobert cheerfully. "That means she will come back."

"I have no brains. I am so filled with my unhappiness, I never noticed it. Thank you, thank you, of course she will come back for her birds."

"She would never leave the birds," said Madame Michel.

"Thank you for coming," said Corti. He moved toward the birds as if he were about to fall with each step. The birds, whom he had never addressed before, became the objects of his intense concern.

He inquired if they had been fed, he put his finger through the bars of their cage and tested the temperature of the water. His face was soggy like a diaper and all the mimicry of arrogance, of man of affairs, of actor and director had left it.

"You have not eaten anything," said Madame Michel. "You have not eaten since yesterday, and while I make you some soup, I will make enough for us all," she said as she left the room.

"In moments like this one turns to one's true friends," said Corti, with an effort at regaining voice and posture, and playing the tragedian. He hobbled to a chair. "She must come back to me."

"She will."

"Why should she?"

"That is the kind of a person she is. 'This place,' she always said, 'is my stable, here is where I belong.'"

"And rightly so, I have always treated her like a dog," Corti said bitterly.

"Some women are happy that way."

"She always said: 'One day I will leave you. One day someone will come whom I will go with.' I am afraid he has come."

"Who?"

"The Professor."

"But he is leaving for America."

172

"And taking her with him."

"No, he is going alone."

"My God, where can she be?"

"Has she anybody to go to?"

"Not that I know of, but the husband is always the last to find out. Oh God."

"But are you sure she left you? She might just have gone for a walk or taken her things to the cleaner."

"No, no, she's gone," mumbled Corti.

"Why?"

"Because of an argument over the car. She was jealous. 'That car,' she said, 'that's all we needed. That car is more important to you than I am. You have more feeling for that damned automobile than for me.'

"And then I got mad and said: 'What else do you expect?' I used some awful words and I said that she was not a wife, not a woman, not a mother, and that she had no sex.'

"Then she said: 'I'm sorry that I have no sex, I can't help that, and I can't help it that I love you. I will always love you, Miomo, but I can't go on living like this, and now it's over. I don't know what I am going to do, but I am leaving you.'

"She cried and said: 'How stupid can one be.' She said that several times and hit the table, the only time she ever made any sort of protest. Then she started packing. I didn't stop her."

He went over again to the birds. Madame Michel came in with a tray.

"Have they been fed?"

"Yes. You asked me that before. I have fed them, as I do every day," said Madame Michel, "and I have also changed the water. But Gala hasn't eaten anything for two days."

"That is a very bad sign," said Corti. "I know women, they are savages. They eat when they are hungry, they drink when they are thirsty, and when they fall in love they burn like bushes. That is what has happened to Gala. She has fallen in love. It came by way of that damned car—that machine—the door was open, the street was open, the driving did it. It came by all the attentions, it came with that dinner at the Tour d'Argent. It's my own fault, I am to blame. I should have never let her out of my sight. She changed from then on. She answered me in another tone. Then that American with the typical and constant imbecility of his kind, the adoration that they all profess toward their mediocre and frigid females, has done more damage than all the rest. The Professor, this and the Professor that. She could not say anything without mentioning his name."

"He was kind to her," said Madame Michel.

"I did not treat her badly, did I? You tell me, honestly," Corti asked of King Dagobert.

Madame Michel was putting down a tray with plates and cutlery. Because the Clochard had no answer, she said:

"No. You could have made her walk the street for you, or sold her to some other Corsican."

"I was strict with her, but I was always correct."

"Except for pulling her by the hair, beating her, slapping her around, insulting her in front of everybody, you were very correct. Of course, what happened in the privacy of this room, what you permitted yourself here, I don't know."

"Nothing happened here that anyone could object to."

"Perhaps that is why she is leaving you," said the Clochard. Madame Michel nodded and slammed the door on her way out.

Kink Dagobert looked at Miomo Corti. "I hope Madame Michel exaggerates."

"No, no," said the breast-beating husband.

"Perhaps you were not strict enough with her and not sufficiently rewarding," said the Clochard.

"You mean I should have beaten her more."

"Well, she sang like a bird, she was happy, I have never seen her cry. She spoke of you as the other of an indissoluble couple, and with respect and affection."

"What are you driving at?"

"When one holds a woman by the whip, then there must also be a reward. The beating, the jealousy, the hair-pulling must be compensated for with passion. If there is a fire, the fire burns and it must be put out and then there is calm and then it starts all over. I mean that perhaps you were not generous enough in that direction."

"You mean—?"

"Yes."

Like one who finally hears his sentence, and gains peace by confession, Miomo Corti dropped his arms. His hands hung down, the palms forward, and he said almost inaudibly:

"Gala is a virgin." Looking out of the window to avoid the Clochard's eyes, he added: "I lived under the impression that everyone knew it, that she had told all the world that I was impotent. That is why I played the role of the tough man so very hard."

"Nobody knows, and nobody suspects, for you are an exquisite actor."

"Forgive me. You knew. She told you? And the Professor? No?"

"She told no one, but I knew."

"How?"

"Oh, I just felt it. There are three virgins on this little island. One is little Lily, the other is up in the Cathedral, and Gala is the third."

"How did you know?"

"Oh, they have the same look."

"Has Gala still?"

"The last time I saw her she had."

"And when was that?"

"An hour ago."

"You saw her an hour ago, and you didn't tell me? You don't mention a word until now? Where was she? What was she doing?"

"She said she had an appointment at the hairdresser at two."

"Oh, thank heaven, now I know where she is. I have made myself unhappy. I have been in such despair. Thank you, thank you. Oh at last someone I can talk to—a true friend."

Miomo Corti looked away, out of the window again.

"I have always been impotent. Imagine what torture that was. I am not even a homosexual. But I have to love someone, so I had to find a creature completely innocent and trusting.

"You know, the sultans and pashas who had their slaves altered to make them into eunuchs had their sex severed and burned, and many died during this operation. But of those that lived the desire for women, for love, was not dead. For love, like joy and pain, resides in the mind, not in the organs. It increases. I loved her more, in all the ways of love that are noble. I prayed to her as to a statue . . . do you understand? I had to find someone to love, someone good, pure, whom I could persuade

176

that sex was dirty, that all its manifestations save those of adoration and love of beauty, of love without passion or selfishness were wrong. The Church aided me a great deal for, by the Virgin birth, they declare all women who beget children normally as unclean and sinful. I searched for years. I found the innocent child, she was like a Hindu idol, and she believed in me and swore that there never would be another man, and then we got married. I never touched her. I transferred the impulses, and succeeded.

"The act of love took place on the stage as on an altar. The undressing, the showing of herself, nude, to those others who were as hungry as I—and the world must be full of them, timid, married to ugly or cold women, lonesome, impotent—all those that are driven here.

"It worked, it released me and her."

Madame Michel entered with the soup. Miomo Corti changed his posture and the subject of conversation.

"It's not worse than any other marriage," he said. "What does one bring to marriage? Security, good manners. Woman respects her husband for the security he offers, his work, his name, for the dignity he lends her. Man respects woman for her domestic virtues. In a household like ours it is not a question of sweeping and cooking, alas.

"We were talking of love. As I have said, it is all in the mind. Take the good Mother Superior who is married to Jesus Christ and for Him has renounced all the pleasures of the world. Is she pale, is she thin? No, she has a comfortable roundness, she is perfectly happy, she has consecrated herself to an ideal. Look at the sweetness of her regard, the pure luminosity, the clarity of her mind."

"Ah yes," said Madame Michel, "but to love Jesus Christ is something very strong and good and a little different and He leaves you in peace."

"Well, I grant you that I am not like Him or an Apostle, not even Judas, but it suffices that one believes. And as far as earthly marriages go, Madame Michel, is your wife longing for your caresses? But since you too have an extraordinary household, let's leave your ménage out of this. But tell me, do you know of any happy marriages, or better, of one happy marriage?"

"Yes, I do," said Madame Michel. "Right down this very street."

Miomo Corti picked up the bottle of Worcestershire sauce and shook it violently and then flavored his soup with liberal squirts.

"You can see," said Madame Michel. "He feels better already."

Miomo Corti picked up his spoon. "Tell us about that happy marriage," he said, putting the spoon in the soup and stirring it. But then he interrupted Madame Michel as a black cloud of misery sank down on him.

"I cannot eat when I think of her not sitting here. Of course there are happy marriages, and as marriages go this one isn't any worse than others."

"Eat your soup," said Madame Michel. The Clochard waited politely. Corti spoke:

"Oh, to wake up with a woman whose beauty has not passed with the night. Here was always this idol, this pure, sweet creature with the grace of youth about her, gentle and kind, and awaking always smiling. This room was like a chapel of love, of adoration."

The room was filled with onion and garlic vapor. King Dagobert sniffed with appreciation.

"What is this heavenly soup made of?" he asked Madame Michel.

"Oh, nothing at all. You take an onion, and a little clove of garlic, and cut them finely and brown them in hot oil. Then you put in small pieces of leftover meat and ham, then tomatoes, cut up, and a bouquet of herbs, a little thyme and basil, a laurel leaf. Then you throw in some rice or a handful of pasta, add a shot of red wine, and you serve it with grated cheese and bread, very simple. You let it cook slowly on a small fire before you throw in the rice and the pasta."

"May I have a little more?" asked Miomo Corti. "And will you tell us about that happy marriage."

"Oh yes, the happy marriage. Madame Carboni, the concierge down the street. You know her, she is the portrait of perpetual happiness, leaning out of her window, framed in geraniums, leaving barely room for her fat cat, whose face is as round as hers. Her bosoms are like children's balloons, her golden waves of hair are bleached blond at home and put up in curlers every week. There are no secrets in this ménage. He drinks, she knits, her face has no lines, her eyes are like two ripe, wet blue plums. She regularly announces, leaning out of her window, to anyone who cares to listen: 'At my age,' she cries, 'he could leave me in peace, at least at seven in the morning.' And he too, with pipe in mouth and his dog following, walks down to his bistro to kill his daily bottle, and he tells you:

'During thirty-five years that I am married to the same woman, neither evening nor morning have I failed in my duty.'"

"Love takes many forms," said Monsieur Corti. "And now we will thank you if you clear away this mess." He had regained his authority.

He passed from the first act, of the ruin, the catastrophe, the hopelessness, to the second act of the drama of the recapture of the innocent. He watched Madame Michel with the kind of eyes that Monsieur Finsterwald would have put into the heads of stuffed tigers.

Madame Michel put the dishes on the tray. She said: "I'm leaving," kicked the door closed behind her, let out a string of curses, laughed, and noisily went on her way down the stairs.

"Dear friend, I need your help desperately. I must get her back," said Corti.

"There is not much time, it is now half-past two." The clockwork of Notre Dame confirmed this.

18.

The Little White Horse

"AH, PAIN AND SORROW OF LOST LOVE," moaned
Miomo Corti. "Life has lost all meaning. I don't exist any more
without her. You must help me."

"I will," said King Dagobert.

"Help me get her back. I am ruined without her. What will
become of this place? I have had a recurrent nightmare, and
that is that I would lose Gala, by illness, by some quirk of fate,
and her loss would be the end of everything, this place and me,
the future, both mine and hers. Now that Aisha is here I have
some insurance, for she will be an attraction like no other. She

181

has authority and power and if she is not the perfect beauty that Gala is she has the devil in her skin, and that always holds an audience.

"I can't afford to lose either. It's like having two wild creatures in cages and if you don't keep them locked up, and under your command and whip, you may never see them again. Women are savages, no matter how sweet they appear."

"Don't worry, she will come back."

"It will be very hard to get her to come back, very hard. There is some champagne in the icebox. Would you mind opening a bottle and pouring some for yourself and me? I am exhausted and nervous, each of my teeth feels as if it were charged with hundreds of volts of electricity. I have lived on pills and champagne, and to mix alcohol with drugs is fatal.

"Every emotion of the theater—doubt, fear of failure—has haunted me. Then came the opening, the taste of success, the feeling of having once more done it, the feeling of money in my pocket. I could not sleep on account of that. I took enough pills to kill a horse. They had no effect, and now that all goes well— this happens. You said she was going to the hairdresser?"

"Yes, she said she was going to the hairdresser."

"That is typical of women. A man can lie dying, but the woman is at the hairdresser's. Well, at least we know where she is. She is serious this time. She has started to move out, she has taken everything except her birds. She is coming back for them and that is my last chance. If I lose her, I can close up shop. I have to kill myself, my life is over." He made a pause. "I know she loves me, and that she really doesn't care about anybody else. You say the American doesn't count and he's leaving?"

"That's right."

"Then there is nobody else."

"There is nobody else," repeated King Dagobert.

"There is one way to get her back, and that is to save my life. You have to help me."

"To commit suicide."

"Exactly, but it must look real or it won't work."

"It must be done very carefully," said the old Clochard.

"Help me. Just this last time. You are easy with words, Dagobert, help me with the farewell note. I have written so many, this must be different. I need pathos, this has to be written in my blood. Give me a line."

"Farewell notes are a waste of time," said the Clochard.

"Perhaps you are right. Well then, we must stage it properly. I must be found at the very last moment. We must time this properly. Here, I'll lend you my wrist watch. I will do it with gas this time. I'll leave the window open just a little so there will be a bit of air. We have to time this closely."

The Clochard shrugged his shoulders and asked when he wanted to do it.

"Now," said Corti. "Thank you, good friend. I will never forget this. Now listen closely. She is at the hairdresser now. In five minutes exactly you call there and give the alarm. The telephone is Samaritaine 5-8364. It takes ten minutes to walk from there to this house or five to run. I assume she will run."

"I am sure she will," said the Clochard.

"Well, anyway a fast walk. As you see her go into this house you alert the police and the hospital. I need the ambulance and the wagon—I need all the props we can get this time, or she will doubt it's real and then it's all for nothing. The neighborhood must know that I am serious, that I am killing myself over her." He took another draft of champagne, emptying the glass. The Clochard refilled it.

"It must smell of gas."

"I will see to that," said the Clochard.

"Now, let's see what time we have, exactly," said Corti. He asked the time by telephone and set his watch. "I think I should leave a note—something like this: 'Now quietly, with my last thoughts, Gala dear heart, you are before my eyes. I have your picture in my hand, and tears fall on it like a gentle rain. This is my last moment. Farewell, dear heart. I cannot give you the life you want. I hope you will be happy. I have no rancor in my soul—'"

"Very good," said King Dagobert. "But we are wasting time."

"Oh look," said Miomo Corti, "here is something else she forgot to take—her little stuffed dog Ton-Ton." He brushed the dog off—it had fallen on the floor—and placed him on the theatrical trunk where he usually stood.

"Now, the bed. I will be found lying here." Miomo Corti started to arrange everything. He took several photographs of girls from a drawer, then he put on his glasses and picked one of Gala.

He kissed the picture and held it in his hand. He turned on the gas. He was about to lie down on the bed, but then looked at the birds in their cage.

"This will do it," he said suddenly. "Her little love birds—I will save them." He got up and opened the window. It was raining outside. He took an umbrella and opened it outside the window and held it over the small cage as he hung it on a nail outside the house.

"This will touch her heart more than any farewell note and she will come back to you," said King Dagobert piously.

"Yes and I will catch my death of cold," said Corti, who was still reaching outside the window busily attaching the umbrella so that the cage of the love birds would be protected. When he had finished Miomo Corti closed the window, as he habitually did.

He looked into the mirror, arranged his necktie. He took a look at his face once more, then he kneeled down and adjusted the jet of the gas heater. Then he lay down on the bed, and from habit he took a cigarette and started to strike a match.

The Clochard said quickly: "Be careful, the gas! Do you want to kill yourself?"

"Thank you, dear friend," said Miomo Corti. "My life is in your hands."

"Now I'd better run."

Miomo Corti took a long breath, and a drink. He smiled and said: "Yes, you better had."

King Dagobert said, "Separate your hands, Miomo, you look so tense," and closed the door carefully behind himself.

It had stopped raining. The taxidermist came running across the wet street, and with him an Arab leading a small, white horse. Ahead of them ran Aisha.

She said: "King Dabobert, we must see Monsieur Corti."

Dagobert barred the entrance of the house. "Not now," he said. "He is sleeping."

"It is really important," said Finsterwald.

"Let him get a little rest, he is exhausted. What can be so important?"

"This horse."

"He must see it to believe it," said Aisha.

"I went with her all the way to the Arab Bidonville, outside Paris, to get it," said Finsterwald. "It belongs to this man. It was in a street circus before all this trouble started and it is a clever little horse with a peculiarity. It loves to untie things. Look at his face, at his mischievous eyes. It's a little Arab stallion. They tie knots in ropes, and he opens them, no matter how complicated, with his large teeth. Now, imagine Aisha on the stage and we dress her like a candy box, with lovely ribbons all over, and Miomo Corti trains this little horse to come in and take a bow and smile like Fernandel, and then start disrobing Aisha by undoing the knots. It will be a sensation."

A flower-vending woman who had a baby cart filled with lilies of the valley approached. "Here," said Finsterwald, handing her a ten-franc note. "Give us a nice large bouquet." Handing it to Aisha he said: "Now you run up, and awaken Monsieur Corti with these flowers."

Fortunately at that moment there appeared Sam Levine, the American tourist, with camera in hand. He held up his hand, smiled, and said: "Hold it, please."

He started a welcome diversion, first photographing Aisha with the bouquet, then Aisha and the flower vendor, then Aisha with the flower vendor and the little white to be in the picture. She was placed on the little white horse, while Sam Levine reloaded his camera. Monsieur Finsterwald now became the director of the production. The Mother Superior came and the group was rearranged, this way and that. Sam Levine exchanged the lens for a wide-angle lens and checked the light and distance.

King Dagobert remained braced in the frame of the door of the house.

The gas of Paris flows slowly and in ancient pipes, mostly of lead, in this quarter of the city. It flows sluggishly during the day, and is at its lowest pressure before mealtime, when everyone cooks. Furthermore, into the calculations of any suicide must go the size of the room, the fact that the windows are leaky as are the doors. Under these circumstances it would take fifteen minutes to accomplish the desired end.

The time mechanism of Notre Dame sounds like the bell of a Swiss village steeple. It now struck off the quarter hour and that made it twenty minutes since Miomo Corti had laid himself down to sleep. King Dagobert left his post. He bought a bouquet of lilies of the valley from the flower woman. The Arab had obtained a piece of rope and tied knots into it and the little white horse undid the knots. Sam Levine reloaded his camera again and measured the light for color film. Now he also photographed King Dagobert and the Mother Superior with the white horse, which smiled. The taxidermist held the horse and the Arab went around, hat in hand, collecting and everyone was glad to give.

19.

Relaxez-Vous

"LOOK, LOOK, sure enough, he's no fool," said Sam Levine, focusing on a young girl in a flowered hat and a summer dress and with bows tied at her back. She had come to admire the white horse and, as if he knew what was expected of him, he got busy and tried to undo a ribbon.

"Perhaps you are right," said Monsieur Finsterwald. "We should not disturb our celebrated expert *de l'intimité féminine* in his sleep. He deserves his rest after all the excitement. This is the month of love and flowers, of the Virgin, of spring, and the day of the lilies of the valley. Oh, where or when has the world been so beautiful!"

"Hold it—stay just as you are," said the tourist to Finster-wald who had his arm around Aisha. "I want to take you two together. Look at each other as you did a moment ago. And then I want to take you, Aisha, with your snake."

"The snake is content," said Aisha. "Ali swallowed a rabbit," she explained, "only yesterday."

"And at last France has swallowed Sam," said Finsterwald. "He will go back to America with thousands of pictures."

"Now a picture of the Mother Superior with Madame Bernard, smile—" *click* "—thank you. Now you take a picture of me," said Sam Levine, handing the camera to Finsterwald.

"Oh, there go my flowers! Stop him! Get him quickly!" cried the flower woman. The little white horse had wandered over to her flower cart and was eating the lilies of the valley and strewing them about.

The Mother Superior and Madame Bernard went to arrange a festive board in the tunnel under the bridge. Lily was helping them. All of them were near tears now. The celebration was for the farewell of Professor Clayborn.

The whole of Paris was in its gayest spring finery, the tender greens of leaves transparent in lukewarm sunlight, the sky a glazed, pale blue tint. Everything delicate, in color, everywhere people with small bouquets of lilies of the valley. The policemen were in their new issue of light capes that were a pale, new, friendly blue, the blue of the French flags. The blue, white, and red flags were fluttering in the breeze, from the Eiffel Tower, from the towers of Notre Dame. Everyone was dressed in his best, all the tourists with camera in hand. The Street Where the Heart Lies was in happy tumult. The flower market from across the bridge had spilled over and there were stands with crocuses and every color of tulip. From the other side of the bridge came the music of a small merry-go-round; the top half of a Ferris wheel could be seen turning. It was spring, and the celebrations of it were everywhere. An artist had set his easel up to do the bridge and was intent on his work while being watched by a dozen tourists.

The street musician sat on the railing and played his concertina. Lily bounced her ball, she bounced it toward the Clochard.

"King Dagobert, please come with me to the fair," she said, "and we'll ride on the merry-go-round and the Ferris wheel. Come, let's go."

She showed him the money Professor Clayborn had given her as a farewell gift. "He said to have a good time with it."

"Yes, Lily, in a little while," said King Dagobert. "Any moment, just a little longer, my child."

The laundress carried napkins down to the table. The bells of Notre Dame started ringing. The music of it stormed into the spring air from open doors.

Then suddenly someone ran out of the Relaxez-Vous and screamed for help. Soon one of the small Renault Paris police cars came racing and four policemen jumped from it. Two stationed themselves at the door of the cabaret, and the other two went inside. The Inspector came running. The Mother Superior left the table she was arranging and she and the laundress went into the house.

"Now," said King Dagobert to Lily. "Come, my child." He

took her by the hand. "Come," he said. "You will get your ice cream and a new ball, and a doll, and ride on the merry-go-round. Come, Lily." He held her by the hand and walked toward the bridge as an ambulance arrived. The Mother Superior looked out of the window of Monsieur Corti's apartment and said to Aisha:

"Miomo Corti has passed away. He is dead." Aisha ran and told Monsieur Finsterwald. The taxidermist yelled after King Dagobert.

"Just one of his jokes," said the Clochard, as he passed the bridge. The taxidermist came after him.

"No, no, I'm afraid it's true, look—" he pointed. Two men were taking a body out of the Relaxez-Vous on a stretcher.

King Dagobert said to Lily: "He is a great actor, Monsieur Corti. If they stick a pin into him, or tickle him, he'll come to life."

Lily said: "Yes, he's only fooling—"

"I'm certain," said the Clochard, "that, if they throw him in the Seine, he'll swim away."

The taxidermist said: "A little respect, please. That man is dead."

"Ah, respect indeed," said King Dagobert, taking off his battered hat.

Lily said: "Is he really dead?"

"Yes, stone dead," said the Inspector.

"Come," said the Clochard, and they went to the other side of the bridge where the music of merry-go-round and Ferris wheel and several other attractions mixed.

"Poor Gala," said Lily.

"Here she comes," said the Clochard.

Gala was in street clothes, in a dark suit, elegantly cut. She wore a blouse buttoned at the throat, she carried a new handbag, and she wore a hat of the latest fashion. An odd parade, led by the Professor, came down the quay to meet her. After him came the street musician with his concertina, then the master plumber of the neighborhood carrying a bidet filled with flowers, and behind him walked what seemed to be a huge, white turtle. As it came out from under the bridge it turned out to be a bathtub upside down, advancing on human hands and feet. Then came the apprentice carrying fixtures for a shower.

Professor Clayborn brought his parade to a standstill as he met Gala. He pointed at the plumbing and bowed.

Clayborn said: "It's for you, a going-away present from me. I remembered that you once said the only thing that you really wanted was a bath and warm water, and so I went and got this for you."

Gala looked into his eyes and took his hands in hers and said: "Thank you, Jeb, thank you. It will be terribly lonesome. I have never been so—" She was about to cry and then she saw the Mother Superior and looked at her sad face and said: "Look at her, she has a face as if someone had died. Nobody wants you to go, Jeb." She still held his hand.

The Mother Superior approached. "Gala," she said, "I can't believe it. It is all over, Gala. He is dead. Miomo is gone. It happened a little while ago, just before you came."

Slowly Gala released Jeb's hand. She stood motionless, her face a blank mask. She did not speak. She did not cry. She did not faint. She just stood in quiet dignity, her eyes focused on nothing.

The laundress said, "Poor Miomo, he had his faults but he

was someone just the same," and being a practical woman she said to the Mother Superior: "We'd better take down the decorations, and I will put the wine back on ice and the food away. We'll have the picnic another day."

The taxidermist said to King Dagobert: "He was an artist. No one can deny that."

The Commissaire de Brigade Mondaine arrived. He was on crutches. He was genuinely touched.

"Allow me to express my condolences, madame. My deepest sympathy. I have lost a good friend."

Everyone around mumbled their condolences.

The bells of Notre Dame rang louder, the music increased in volume, and a man came in haste, a dour, dark man—the one who makes the last arrangements.

"Which one is the widow?" he asked.

Aisha, who stood in the frame of the door, with Ali wound around her, said: "Ah?"

The man had seen the head of the python and recoiled. He repeated his question and Aisha pointed to the group of people surrounding Gala. The undertaker presented himself to the Commissaire.

The Commissaire said: "This is Madame Corti."

The laundry woman wailed: "He is hardly dead when these black beetles come running."

The undertaker removed his hat.

"Where have they taken my husband?" Gala asked. These were the first words she had spoken since the Mother Superior had told her that Miomo was dead.

"He is at the morgue," said the Commissaire. "But don't go there, he looks terrible. Poor Miomo. He was all life and excitement when I left him yesterday, and now only the misery is there. Your little birds are safe, I have them at the commissariat."

The undertaker put his hat back on and with pad and pencil in his hand he said:

"Madame, I am sorry, but I must have some kind of instructions. I beg your pardon for addressing these questions to you at this moment, but it must be done, it is urgent. What kind of a burial shall we provide?"

The Commissaire shouted at the undertaker:

"You are of the neighborhood, you knew Corti, you know of his circumstances. It's like taking a bed away from a bankrupt to ask anything by way of a funeral except the cheapest kind of burial. You know that!"

Gala said: "What do you permit yourself? What do you mean by bankrupt? We always paid our bills, we owe no one."

The Commissaire pleaded: "No offense, madame, I merely wanted to protect you against this ghoul. They always get you at a moment like this, when people are overwhelmed with sorrow and unable to make a sound decision."

Gala said: "I know very well what I am doing."

The Commissaire wiped his brow. He said:

"Yes, I know, dear lady. I only meant that we are all friends, and can speak freely, and we know that this life of strip tease, cabaret, jazz, and bar-keeping offers no security, and alas, that poor Miomo had expensive tastes." He turned to the undertaker and said:

"Run along. Do the necessary. Get together a priest and an altar boy, ring the bells, and have it over with."

Gala, in a fury, said to the undertaker:

194

"I want a first-class funeral for my husband."

The undertaker said: "Very well, madame. Now as for the details, how shall we dress him? There is a very good formal paper shirt. It looks like the best starched linen."

Gala cut him short: "Did you understand what I said? My husband is to be dressed properly, as he was in life. My husband had his shirts made to measure and with his monogram at the Rue Castiglione."

As she talked, her mouth began to lose shape. She said:

"Dress him in his best. There is a shirt — I have it — he wore for the opening. He was especially proud of it. It was made by Battistoni, in the Via Condotti in Rome. A fine shirt with ruffles. I'll get it, it's just newly ironed."

She turned to Clayborn and put her head on his shoulder. He embraced her.

Gala said to him: "Forgive me, and have a little patience, Professor, for at one time I loved him."

20.

Celebration

THE MARTIAL FIGURE in magnificent vestments, the authoritative marshal who keeps order in the interior of French churches and who is called *"Un Suisse,"* most probably after the Swiss guards on duty at the Vatican, led the procession from the altar of Notre Dame to the portal.

Outside the sun shone, the sky was blue, the flags of France were sailing in the breeze and all the assembled people of the neighborhood were smiling.

In the case of Gala and Jeb, it was easy. Once the wedding ceremony was over, the bride, dressed in a severe, high-buttoned white brocade gown designed by Yves St. Laurent, came out of Notre Dame. She held the bouquet in her right hand, and put her left arm through that of the happy bridegroom. They stopped and smiled for the photographers with Lily, the flower girl, who was also dressed in white. Then the cortege moved on. First came the witnesses, King Dagobert and the Mother Superior. Then Herr Doktor Ueberlinger, who finally got to kiss the bride, the still limping Commissaire de Brigade Mondaine, and several members of the commissariat lent the glory of gala uniforms to the occasion. There was all the *beau monde* of Paris and, most important, the human dynamo Signor Vivanti. These were followed by the friends of the neighborhood and onlookers.

IN THE CASE OF AISHA AND FINSTERWALD, there had been many complications.

In France there are several documents required before a marriage can take place. One of the most important is *"La Justification du domicile, où de la résidence."* This paper is obtained by the *Commissaire de Police.* It must state where you have resided for the last six months, and must be attested to by the landlord or concierge of the building in which you live.

The second is, *"L'acte de naissance."* Finsterwald was born in Warsaw, but he had no proof of that. It was long ago, and he was without a country. As for Aisha—

"Where were you born?"

"Ah?"

"Who was your father?"

"Ah?"

"Who was your mother?"

"I don't know."

"What was your mother's maiden name?"

"Ahhh?"

Aisha looked like someone coming out of deep water for air. She had her mouth open, but nothing came out of it.

"We will have to invent it," said Finsterwald. "Let us put down that you were born in Marrakech or Oran. Your father's name was what?"

"Mahomet."

"Yes, but Mahomet what? Give me a good Arabian name. Let's look in the papers or ask somebody."

Number three, "*Un certificat médical.*"

The act of the fifteenth of April 1946 demands that applicants for a marriage license must be accompanied by a medical certificate not older than two months, attesting to their health, which is to be supported by "*les examins radiologique et sérologique.*" This also is to be legalized by the *Commissaire de Police.* There is then the question of Article 37 of the code of French nationality which says that a woman of another country who marries a Frenchman acquires French nationality at the moment of the celebration of the marriage. *Merde alors,* that complicates things all over again, for the groom has no nationality, and neither has the bride. They are both legally nonexistent. But Monsieur Finsterwald had the certificate of the landlord that he has lived in the house at Number 19 on The Street Where the Heart Lies for a number of years and is an exemplary tenant.

What then?

"I love you, Aisha, and you love me. That is enough."

They tore up the papers and threw them into the municipal

wastebasket of Room 1134 of the Bureau of Marriages and Civil Status and he carried her across the threshold of his home.

"Just the same," said Madame Bernard, "it will be difficult, this *ménage*. Will she sit on the floor or learn to balance on a chair, or will he sit on the floor with her?

"Will she wash her hands before coming to the table? Will they eat couscous and lamb for the rest of their lives, and will she eat with her fingers, or be fed with his or hers while love is new? And how will they walk? At first she walked in back of him. He tried to make her walk at his side, but somehow she couldn't do that, so now she runs ahead of him. That is the modern way the Arabs do it in Algeria. They let their women run ahead on account of the land mines.

"And the snake. Are they going to keep it in the house like a cat, or a dog? Incidentally, when a snake does its business, how does that happen?"

Nobody knew.

Only Madame Michel was optimistic. "What does it matter? Let them be happy, for heaven's sake," said Madame Michele lightheartedly, arranging the table for the wedding feast. "I will teach her to do some simple good dishes, I will help her to get dressed. Now we will get ready for the wedding dinner."

The table was set down under the bridge, chairs were brought from everywhere, nothing was forgotten. The champagne was cooled in the bathtub, the red wine was in the baby carriage, together with brandy and *Marc de Bourgogne* and the Sweet William pear distillate.

Madame Bernard's laundry served as a kitchen. It was a matter of patience now, awaiting the arrival of the wedding party. The menu was:

BRIOCHE AU FOIE GRAS
ASPIC OF LOBSTER
CHICKEN À LA KING IN A CASSEROLE AND RICE

and besides

ASSORTED SANDWICHES

for bystanders and the musicians.

STUFFED OLIVES

Raw celery, carrots, things to nibble on for Herr Doktor Ueberlinger.

BABA WITH FRUITS AU KIRSCH
TWO WEDDING CAKES

Orangeade and citronade for the children.

"And at last I have my return ticket to America," said Sam Levine to King Dagobert. "Tomorrow, by jet, vous comprenez? American go home."

"I understand," said King Dagobert. "You may speak English to me, I understand perfectly well. You are the happy American, you love your country, and your work, and your family. I envy you. We will drink to America and your happiness." The King poured champagne, and standing up they toasted the United States.

"You are very fortunate," said King Dagobert.

"Oh, I have my troubles too," said Sam Levine. "That is, I

had — my kid — but now he's all straightened out. Kennedy did it. He needed more soldiers."

Madame Michel said: "They're supposed to be back now. Everything will be ruined."

"Don't worry," said the King. "They'll get here in time."

Madame Bernard was in conversation with Madame Michel concerning Aisha and she said:

"You know, Monsieur Finsterwald told me he had said to Aisha: '*Je vous aime,*' and Aisha answered: '*Moi aussi.*' So he was very happy and asked: '*Vous aussi?*' and she answered: '*Oui, moi, aussi je m'aime.*'"

"Ha ha," King Dagobert exclaimed to Sam Levine. "Finsterwald said to Aisha: 'I love you.' She said: 'Me too,' so he was beside himself and asked her: 'You love me?' and she said: 'I too love myself.' That is how that romance started."

"Well, at least she's honest," said Sam Levine.

And then the laundress said: "Translate for him when at the *commissariat* they asked her: 'Can you read and write?'"

The King said: "She answered: 'Write to whom? Read what?'"

"That is formidable and profound," said the King.

"The little woman knows her mind," said Sam Levine, and the laundress observed:

"None of that worries Monsieur Finsterwald, not in the least. He is struck dumb and blind with love. He sits and helps her peel the snake. Aisha said: 'Poor Ali, he has no trees, he needs the bark of trees to scrape off his skin, he is shedding.' So they go out to the Bois de Boulogne and sit under a tree with rough bark, and Ali slides up into the branches. Such is love in Paris, you can see the most remarkable things happening."

"Tell me about your boy and President Kennedy who needed more soldiers," the King said to Sam Levine, filling his glass.

"It's a gruesome thing to watch," continued the laundress, "these two sitting, peeling the snake, she dark as an Arab, in her white sheets, and he pale as a piece of sugar. And the snake—they do it like children picking scabs off themselves, or skin from sunburn from their noses."

"Madame, please," said the King, "we are about to eat."

"The kid you ask me about," said Sam Levine. "Well, sometimes your kids surprise you. Well, going into the army was what I didn't want for him—he's a smart kid. So he comes in and says: 'I don't want them to send me some place to be a grease monkey' and he says that's that, he's done it—he enlisted.

"We always worried about his eyes, he's nearsighted. Then he got the call, so they sent him to Georgia, a state in the South, to a supply depot. You understand? That's how life is. I used to get mad every morning. I get up early on my day off, at six. I take a four-minute shower, breakfast is on the table, and I'm off to do some work around the house, or in the garden. The kid is still in bed. It always made me mad, but I didn't say anything to his mother. I told him a few times but without any effect.

"Well, he gets a furlough from the army and comes home. He's learned a lot. On my day off, he's up. When I come down, he says: 'Pop, I've got a schedule. By six I have my shower, I'm shaved, and I've got my own bed made.' Best thing that ever happened. Now, isn't it funny that they tell you something like that with pride when they never listened to you?"

"Here comes the wandering bedsheet," said Madame Bernard.

That was the name in general use for Aisha, not with malice,

202

but rather with a mixture of compassion and that French compulsion to put things in some category. Aisha was no longer in a sheet but in a gray suit, and trotted ahead, held, as if a busy little tug were pulling a boat, by the outstretched hand of Finsterwald.

Everyone welcomed them. "She's as beautiful as a black swan," said the King. "A black swan in white plumage."

They held each other by the hand, and, since they had made every effort to legalize their status and only the law was against them, the neighborhood accepted them as a married couple entitled to respect.

"So here we are waiting until that damned boat gets back," said Finsterwald.

"He invited us too," said Madame Bernard, "but we chose to stay with you, and besides there was all the work. Sit down."

They sat—and they waited. And they talked. About the beautiful wedding. About the colorful spectacle at the quay side. About the flowers in Notre Dame. About funerals.

"Yes, yes," said the Clochard, "here in France we have a great feeling for ceremony, for pageantry. We buried Napoleon that way, and great poets and artists. And properly so."

"I will never forget dear Christian Dior's funeral," said the Mother Superior. "Three bus loads of police to keep order. The streets blocked, the church transformed into a flower garden—that is what the wedding reminded me of. The Duchess of Windsor and other great ladies, and in the center there were the peasants from his native village.

"Now, who thought of bringing them, who was so kind to make it possible for them to come, and to have the best places, close to him? They were crying, and kissing each other, and looking about in astonishment. For the first time in their lives in Paris, and for the last. And then the beautiful words the priest said."

"What did he say, good Mother? Tell us, please," asked Monsieur Finsterwald.

"The good Father said: 'No, we need not worry about the departed because he is happy, for he stands before the throne of the Almighty, because he was a good man, a pure man, and now he is already busy dressing the angels.' At this some of the peasants laughed, some of them cried, but one could not tell which, for their faces were so simple."

The Mother Superior went into the laundry to help Madame Bernard with the preparations.

"What time is it?" asked the Mother Superior, who owned no watch.

"When we got painted," said Madame Bernard, "they took the clock away and haven't brought it back yet. Workingmen aren't dependable at all these days. Things like that never happened before. But there, listen—" Notre Dame tolled the hour. It was five.

The taxidermist talked to Herr Doktor Ueberlinger, and to Madame Michel, who was also among those who had not received the engraved, much sought after invitations to the boat trip on the Seine. Finsterwald said in his scofflaw manner:

"Ah, that is rich. He stands at the throne of the Almighty and already occupies himself dressing the angels. Well, if Miomo Corti stands at the heavenly throne now, we know what he is doing to the angels, he is undressing them."

Madame Michel came to Miomo Corti's defense. She said: "I doubt very much if dear Miomo is there, but if he is, it will cost the good Lord a great deal less than what Monsieur Dior would do to them if he is there."

"Yes," said Doktor Ueberlinger, "let us pray for the good Lord. He must have his troubles in the afterlife, more even than he has here."

"You know," said Finsterwald, "I stuffed a llama once for Monsieur Dior and dyed it in silver for a fashion show, and a golden gazelle for the window of his boutique. I met him several times. He was an extraordinary person, kind of what you'd imagine a Byzantine Pope to be like, very knowing, soft-spoken, and unmovable. You know the genius of Monsieur Dior consisted in finding le bon Dieu here on earth. He found him in Monsieur Boussac, who is rich rich rich. He has a lot of money, as much as all the simple and good weeping peasants in France have hidden in gold in their socks—and that is in the milliards."

The King walked down the embankment to look toward the bend from which the bridal barge was expected.

"Was he a good man?" asked the Herr Doktor.

"What is that, 'a good man'? He was no worse than the others, and he paid his bills. I saw that funeral also. Of course with different eyes than the good Mother Superior."

"I think they are coming. I hear music," shouted the King.

"Be careful of the paint. You have some blue on your freshly starched, beautifully snow white headdress," said Madame Bernard to the Mother Superior.

"No, it's not them," called the King from the river.

"It will be night before they get back. Where have they gone to?" asked the Mother Superior. She walked down to the river also. Little Lily came bouncing her ball.

"To go back to the funerals of couturiers, et cetera," the taxidermist observed. "Isn't it curious, when you think of it, that the majority of these kind of men, who have really no love for women, no physical desire for them, who really detest them and make no secret of it, are in the frantic business of dressing them up, doing their hair, making them beautiful."

"Yes," said Madame Michel. "Very odd, a curious breed, the men employed in women's wear."

"In the mass of people at the interment of Monsieur Christian Dior," said Finsterwald, "there were various bouquets of fairies crying—large and small groups of them—just simple needle-and-thread boys—also the eminent ones in fashion and those in the arts and the government, all letting their tears run down their cheeks unashamed, without handkerchiefs. There can't have been any tears left in Paris that day.

"There were some of them so pale their faces looked like dirty newspapers. Their mascara was running down over their cheeks and they were covered with blotches and smears. And one of his best friends, the one who looks like a dead bullfighter, had a handkerchief, a very fancy one with a black border, and was weeping into this. It was a holiday for the photographers.

"The mannequins, however, in mourning in their own fashion, didn't wear any maquillage on that sad day. They were neat and dry.

"Oh, the funeral of a couturier!"

"When you think of fashion," said Madame Michel, "and that for five thousand years the human form has remained the same, only dressed one way or another—do this, do that, let it in, let it out, take it off, put it on, lift it, take it down, a pair of scissors, a needle and thread, and swatches of material and the fuss they make over it! It's infantile this profession."

"Let's drop it," said the taxidermist, "here comes the King. He doesn't like complications about anything."

The King looked at the two. "When will they come? The newlyweds?" he asked, looking up the river and looking at Doktor Ueberlinger's watch, which, like all things Swiss, worked properly and told the exact time to the second and also the date. So much had happened on that flower-scented wedding day.

21.

The Friend of
The Family

THE PROBLEMS OF A MAN like Signor Vivanti are those of
the devil, his work is never done. The hunt for women is never
over in men assigned to this pursuit by nature. The details are
curious and the moves of endless variety, like in complicated
chess games.

The Roman office of Signor Vivanti, in the Palazzo Vivanti,
was the scene of his heartache, it echoed to his groans and
curses. He knew he was an idiot and behaved like one, he was as
if covered by poisonous gelatin. He looked like a decomposed

fish. In moments of stress he choked himself by holding tight to the flabby skin under his powerful head. He almost suffered a coronary a day.

He tried to pull himself together but could not conduct his business in his normal, dynamic fashion. He sat on the edge of his executive chair under the great chandelier, with his trusted secretary, both looking hopelessly into space. This state had taken hold of him since the funeral of Miomo Corti, just when things seemed to be right. He had sent immense tributes of flowers, not to the departed, for he was a practical man, but to the widow. He had commuted between Rome and Paris, neglected his wife and sons, all for the beautiful widow. On his first visit, he played the strong man.

"No more of this nonsense," he had said.

He had stumbled into the Relaxez-Vous in a dark suit and turning his black hat in his hand, and offered his counsel, his services, his life—and diamond-and-black-pearl earrings from Van Cleef and Arpels with his companionship—all in his pouncing fashion—all in the morbid state of the desperate man. Now that Miomo Corti was no longer, after a decent passage of time and a divorce from his wife, they could get married. He hoped that perhaps she would consent to. No? Well, then in that case he had come to offer his love, his support, his advice, a villa outside of Rome, his lifelong devotion. He proposed voyages—around the world—to India—a codicil in his will making her forever secure. No? A change of air then, a trip, a small journey to America? Or journeys to the environs of Paris to help her forget? He had come to stand by her. He spoke always urgently, driven, seated forward on the chair, his fat legs under his stomach, his eyes bulging, his throat in his worried hand. A spasm of heavy breathing came over him whenever she said, "No."

The doctor had forbidden him any kind of strain or excitement. He said she was killing him. He could not live without her. Would Gala have dinner with him? At the Tour d'Argent?

"No, thank you, you are very kind," said Gala to the poor unhappy monster, and put her hand on his thick heavy wet one. She was very sorry. She could not go out with him. She was not thinking of a career, or a villa. No, she could not marry him, nor entertain thoughts of any liaison or arrangement with him. She had very definite plans.

His eyes were on her face in utmost desolation. He suffered and flew back to Rome. She was in love. Terrible. An incredible catastrophe.

When he finally accepted the unhappy fact, his entire metabolism underwent an upset. The tortured eyes became permanent fixtures of his face, a dreadful sound like a bad telephone connection started a humming in his internal ears, he fought loss of balance, and gasped for air. He added an analyst to his doctor, a rare thing in Italy, and saw them both daily. He took relaxing medicines, he wanted to die.

All this for beauty. Why is it that no one has any sorrow, or loss of heartbeat, for a plain woman, with nice hair, a nose in the middle of her face, and honest eyes like his wife's? Why does one suffer only for the beautiful, for the unattainable?

"Because beauty is health and health is desirable for nature's plan of reproduction." That is the way the good Herr Doktor Ueberlinger explained it to Signor Vivanti. "She is going to marry the Professor."

"Oh God." Now she again became many degrees more beautiful as she went further out of reach. But Vivanti was not one to give up easily.

Again he came and went back to Rome and sat in his Mussolini chair and dictated cables and letters, and made important decisions. He did all this like a pilot in an instrument landing. In the forefront of his vision, on the windshield, there was ever present the face of Gala.

He grabbed his throat again.

The way to do it, he said to himself, as he dined that night with his wife and two sons, was to play the waiting game. Treat the whole matter like the man of the world he was. And so he turned his sorrow-filled eyes from the painting of Judith with the head of Holofernes that hung in his dining room and that he had been staring through, and focused on the food. A *bollito* was being served and he wanted a slice of chicken, a slice of sausage, a slice of beef. After all, there were nuances and he was not a boy any more sobbing his sorrow into his pillow into the night. "And some more wine," he said.

"Si, signore."

"What were you talking about?" he asked his wife. "I didn't hear for a moment."

There was a conversation going on between mother and sons about the dentist who had brought some electric toothbrushes from Switzerland. They did not work on the Italian current, but one could use them with a battery.

"Is there any other topic," barked Signor Vivanti, annoyed, "than to talk about brushing your teeth at the dinner table?"

They changed the topic.

"The way to do it," said Vivanti, speaking to himself, "is to wait until she marries that oaf of an Americano, and gets tired of being a housewife. The way to do it is to become a friend of the family, to be a friend to the husband, to attend the wedding, to give them a party, a wonderful surprise party, yes." He smiled for the first time in a long time. To be the godfather of the first-born. Gala was young, she would still be beautiful, maybe more so, and he would wait and come to the rescue.

The signal with which they got up was awaited. Papa folded his napkin neatly, the butler pulled back his chair. He had some work to do, he said, and would go to his office. He kissed his wife, his sons dutifully kissed him, and all except the good Italian Mamma went out to pursue their various mischiefs. Vivanti was on the telephone to Paris. He wanted to find out when the happy event would occur. He would be allowed, would he, to assist at the wedding?

Oh yes, said the dear girl. She was so happy to channel his adoration properly into Notre Dame.

And would she allow him to give them a little present by way of a party after?

Well, they had some old and close friends who had invited them for dinner.

Oh, of course he understood and would not take too much of their time, just a small fiesta, al fresco, for old times' sake, to wish them all the happiness in this world. Well, to that they could not say no.

The eyelids of Signor Vivanti functioned properly again, his pulse, blood pressure, and breathing were almost normal under the welts of fat, his heavy heart labored no longer.

He told his secretary to get a plane for Paris.

It is not generally known that one can hire the *bateaux*

mouches which travel up and down the Seine for private functions. Now that would be novel. A party on a ship. The ship would wait at the quay in front of Notre Dame, the wedding guests and the invited would come on board. There would be music and champagne. The gigantic Vivanti machine went into action with attention to all details. He wanted a production larger than *La Dolce Vita*, a fiesta to bedazzle Paris, to make Notre Dame proud and make it turn around as the bridal barge passed.

"Get me the boat, get me the Republican Guard, get me the world's best decorator, get that Clochard dressed up—" nobody must be forgotten "—get Herr Doktor Ueberlinger, get me a carpet firm, get me the best florist, invite everybody that matters. Get me the Chancellery, get me the Cardinal of Paris, get me De Gaulle, get me Georges of the Ritz, get me the American Ambassador, get me, get me, get me—

"Ah, alors, the Clochard won't come out from under his bridge, and De Gaulle won't come. The boat we have, everything else is in order."

"Calmez-vous, relaxez-vous," said Herr Doktor Ueberlinger, who was now working on the various humps and bumps that constituted the body of Signor Vivanti. "Here are sketches from the decorator."

In one of them the *bateau mouche* was transformed into a Nile barge, in another into a floating bouquet with white and yellow flowers. Peppermint-sticklike effects were made in silk of all the stanchions, ventilators were painted yellow and white, white cockatoos were placed here and there and sat decoratively with their yellow combs raised like endive salad. Yellow and white, the Papal colors, the most becoming and the most luminous.

"That is what I have decided on," said the great man, stabbing the paper three times. "That is it. Put it in work. And I want the Cathedral lined with white and yellow roses, chrysanthemums, yes, and an orchestra, elegant, and the best band. We will pick up the party at the door of the Cathedral. I want it all on film. I want a special platform where they board the boat. There is a wide stone stairway down to the water. I want the Republican Guard there." His secretary inquired what he wanted the Republican Guard for. "In full dress, with sabers drawn, from the portals of Notre Dame down to the boarding platform, one every two feet on both sides.

"Then we cruise up and down the Seine, until dusk. Then we go past Notre Dame and the Ile de la Cité, and we stop in front of The Street Where the Heart Lies, and there at the quay in front of their house we stop—the voyage is ended—*basta.*"

The details in a plan by Signor Vivanti were always carried out and everyone conformed, including the weather. It was a lovely day. The guests were happy. The sultan said to a Rothschild: "Curious how it changes their whole personality. Look at Gala. Since she has become a married woman, an hour ago, all has changed. What a pity. She was so gay." It was a lovely cruise, for all except the bride and groom, who wanted to be alone.

There was one slight miscalculation. Someone had forgotten to check the capacity of the sanitary facilities of the bateau mouche, the boat called *Tristan.* In its normal use a men's room with facilities for two men, and the same for ladies, were ample, but burdened with a party of 250 people who consumed a great many cases of champagne, whisky, gin, and punch, there was a sudden urgency and rush. A queue formed and there was near panic.

In the case of the male passengers this was relieved by the fact that this water journey took place in France. The men eventually went to the back of the boat to the lower deck, and for a while it looked like the fountains in the Place de la Concorde playing.

For the women it was a more serious matter. But then in France nobody cares much about how they solve problems of such urgency and while the streets are dotted with kiosks for the convenience of gentlemen, no one cares about the ladies' needs.

The *Tristan* finally turned and passed under the iron bridge which connects the Ile St. Louis with the Ile de la Cité, and then it turned left again and slowed and came to a halt, facing The Street Where the Heart Lies, and there the farewells and thanks were said, while the band played.

The generous Signor Vivanti was near tears. He waved goodbye, and the lovely ship floated on, and, blowing its horn, disappeared under the next bridge. "Thank God, that's over," said both bride and groom and disappeared for a while.

22.

Long Past Your Bedtime

"Ah, and now, at long last, we are just us, the families at table."

It was still light enough and Sam Levine climbed around and photographed the party. People came bearing gifts, and most of the things that the Professor had thrown out of his window reappeared. And, by subscription, the friends had bought a new mattress.

"Incidentally, I have repaired your typewriter, and also your binoculars," said Monsieur Finsterwald to the Professor. "They work perfectly."

"Thank you, thank you," said Gala who had sent a vacuum cleaner as a wedding gift to Aisha. It surprised Ali at first as it had a long, snakelike tube, which the reptile mistook for a drab, gray relative. Aisha was intelligent. She sat at the left of the King, and watched how he took fork in hand and cut through the slice of crust and goose liver paste and she did the same.

"It will all come out all right," said Madame Michel, watching her. "Pauvre petit chou, drink now."

"Yes, we drink to both brides and grooms, and *Vive la France,*" said the good-will ambassador from New York.

"Yes, and *Vive le General De Gaulle,*" said the Commissaire, "and *Vive le Président Kennedy,* and *Vive l'Astronaut.*"

"This exploit of *le gallant astronaut c'est merveilleux. Bravo, pour l'Amérique,*" said Madame Michel. The bystanders took that up.

Madame Michel had been steadily fortifying herself with *eau de vie,* her favorite drink.

"Isn't anybody going to toast Miomo?" she asked. "Poor Miomo without whom none of this happiness would be possible."

The King raised his glass.

"To Miomo."

"May he rest in peace," said the Mother Superior.

The Professor was in a reflective mood. With his arm around Gala he looked up at the sky which was a crystal pure evening blue and he said:

"*Miomo und die Notwendigkeit des Bösen.*"

"What does that mean?" asked Gala.

"It's German. It means the necessity of evil."

"He was a wonderful man," said Madame Michel.

"He wasn't evil—Miomo," said Gala.

The King said: "He was evil, but he did not know it. He was what he was and had to be, and he had to bear the burden of it. Few people have pity for the devil."

"What is he talking about?" asked Sam Levine, taking a flash picture of the King leaning back and brushing his beard with his hands.

The Professor said: "Well, it's something like this. You take Khrushchev, he's not happy-making, but he was created by nature to do a certain task, like Miomo Corti. If there were no Khrushchev, there would be no astronaut, no trip to the moon."

"It's too deep for me," said the American tourist.

Aisha looked at her husband with a questioning expression.

He said: "I will explain it to you, chérie, my love. Man came out of the sea, out of the primeval ooze, and to survive he had to fight heat and cold, wild animals, water, fire, stones, and sand. And this was very difficult, but he survived. The strongest survived and conquered the elements. Then, when man had conquered nature, man fought man, and again the strongest survived. And the cold war, as it is called, the tension between East and West, is a master plan of nature. On that account we can fly to New York in six hours, because the Americans built jet planes, and on that account the astronaut can fly around the earth in an hour and a half, and soon we will be able to go to the moon, and the other planets. You understand?"

Aisha opened her mouth and said:

"Ah!"

She had not taken her eyes from his, and not understood a word, but she had listened with the rapt attention with which most wives listen to the lifelong discourses of their mates.

The wedding cakes were cut. Eventually the guests departed. The two married couples went to their homes. The onlookers faded away, the table was cleared. Madame Bernard took back her linen, Madame Michel carried the dishes, the crockery, and the empty bottles back.

"Lily," said the Mother Superior, "you are still up? It's long past your bedtime. Come along."

Up above in their home, Gala and the Professor held onto each other for dear life, and between embraces he said to his wonderful wife as they stood at the large window:

"Look, Gala, how beautiful. And listen —" Jeb pointed up to the Cathedral of Notre Dame, which had just emerged from darkness. Bathed in floodlights and music, it floated in the night sky.

The golden angel with its trumpet and the many saints that stood on its roof were magically brought to life and glowed as if made of transparent emerald jade. The full orchestra and voices rose, the huge ship of the spirit, and of God, floated in the Paris sky.

Below, the Mother Superior started her motor scooter. Little Lily jumped on the back seat. They waved good-bye to the King, and rolled away. The production of sound and music came to an end, the sacred concert thinned out into a lacework of echoes. The light of the moon and the stars and of the street lamps took over, and of Notre Dame there was now left only a design etched into darkness — an outline made of luminous spiders' threads stood there in the night.

"Look down there, Jeb," said Gala. "What is that white thing below under the bridge, next to the King?"

The Professor took his binoculars and looked. There was the baby carriage, and the Clochard.

The kinglike figure with his strong white beard sat there as he always had, leaning against the stone arch. The moisture that rose from the Seine softened all contours and colors. The old man's cloak shone like blue velvet, he wore his hat like a crown. On the Professor's old mattress slept the Arab, and at the foot of it, the little white horse had lain down. It was like a picture out of the Bible.

Books Forming a Series
By and About Ludwig Bemelmans

Other Titles in Preparation

Louis Bemelmans

Bemelmans tales overflow with whimsical eccentrics, somber head waiters, and a long string of charmingly irresponsible and wholly unlikely people and situations. The plots of his stories lead to improbable solutions. We accompany him through western Europe and Latin America, and we learn first hand from this master writer and illustrator of existing warmth in people and places. His exuberance for life and humanity creates nostalgia, a fresh glow and a yearning for more of the same. His writings and book illustrations brim over with light-hearted satire and joyful humor. In short, Bemelmans makes us feel good.

This book was composed in
Cochin and Nicholas Cochin Black
by The Sarabande Press, New York.

It was printed and bound by
Arcata Graphics Company, New York
on 60# Sebago cream white antique paper.

The typography and binding were designed by
Beth Tondreau Design, New York.

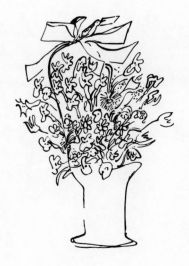